NEWBIE

Also by Tali Nay

Schooled

Jeweled

Fooled

NEWBIE

Tali Nay

corner
chapter
press

NEWBIE
Copyright © 2019 Tali Nay

For further information, please contact
Corner Chapter Press,
PO Box 21752, Cleveland, OH 44121

Book Cover and Interior Design by VMC Art & Design LLC

Published in the United States of America

ISBN: 978-0-9914986-3-5
Library of Congress Control Number: 2019908494

To Lizzie,
for her one-way ticket and big dreams,
and for inspiring me always.

I wouldn't have wanted a New York without her.

Author's Note

I'M NOT ONE OF THOSE GIRLS WHO CLAIMS NEW York City as her own just because she once lived there. True, I did live there for a brief time while pursuing a particular dream, but that is not to say that I experienced anywhere near all the things available in such a vast and vibrant city. What I noticed, however, even from my short stint as a city girl, was that living in New York City for *any* amount of time is bound to produce stories and memories that could come from no other place. And while I always felt like a newbie when it came to city life, I did it. I moved there. I lived there. I fulfilled a dream there.

If the two time arcs in this book confuse you, watching a movie called "The Last Five Years" might help. While the arcs in the movie each represent a different character, one moving from end to beginning and the other recalling the same events but moving from beginning to end, the two arcs in this book are obviously both me. Still, I've always wanted to write a book this way, where you know the ending even from the very beginning. There's something irresistible to me about the repeated contrast between finality and hope. Between how you *think* it's going to go and how it actually does.

As in all of my books, I rely on my own memories and journals to recall the stories I tell. Everything is true and accurate according to my own recollection, which, I admit, may at times be flawed. But it's the best I can do. If you were involved in any of these stories and remember them differently, I hope you'll understand.

NEWBIE

GOING

WHEN I LEFT NEW YORK, I TURNED TO JOAN Didion. This was nothing unusual, having done the same in other pivotal life situations that left me with more feeling than I knew what to do with. Honestly, sometimes simply glancing at that 1968 picture of Didion and the Corvette is enough to convince me of what I should do. Or at least convince me that I should start smoking.

Goodbye to all that.

The whole crux of moving away from New York City leaves a person feeling a rather torturous combination of emotions. I sat outside on the steps of my building trying to pinpoint what mine were.

While sitting, I noticed that the small piece of cardstock I'd taped outside the doorframe when I moved in with instructions on delivering packages to apartment 6 had completely faded in the sunlight. I took the cardstock down and ran my fingers over the surface, glancing down to where the steps met the sidewalk, where the sidewalk became street, and then down to where my street met up with the vein of other streets that connected me to this crazy island I'd been inhabiting.

I'd read Didion's iconic essay, as well as the collection of essays bearing the same title, all written by authors who'd lived in and then left New York. It's full of the things you'd expect to hear, like how sad these authors were to be leaving the city; how there's simply nothing quite like living in Manhattan. How they would be or in fact *were already* a bit bored now living in their sleepy little beach towns, even if those beach towns did prove more conducive to other pursuits. Like family life. Or even just life.

I understood this sadness all too well. I'd made a list in preparation for my departure with all the New York City things I wanted to do, or do again, before I left the city, and my recent weeks had been an absolute study in epicness. I was in awe of the city. Of the lights and the crowds, the history and culture, the food, the diversity. The accessibility of everything. And I would never have this again.

Goodbye to all that.

Yet when I thought about those four words, when I held them in my mind like the worn cardstock now in my hands and pictured Manhattan as past instead of present, what I felt most wasn't sadness. It was relief.

How shameful, and also confusing. Because I'd wanted to live here. I'd wanted it all my life. And yet it has to be said: New York City is its own kind of stress. That's not a groundbreaking statement, but this specialized city stress is affecting. And people feel it differently, and to different degrees. I'd felt it more than I would have predicted, and certainly more than I ever let on, both to those here with me as well as those reading my letters back home. Sitting there on those Harlem steps in the early summer sun, what became clear then was that in addition to relief, what I felt most upon leaving the city was failure.

Because I was not cut out for this.

And yet I had wanted to be. So much.

But who among us has not wanted things she ultimately can't sustain? Or, worse, chooses not to, despite the want.

So I had lived in New York without ever feeling truly relaxed about it. So I had perhaps never fully unpacked my bags. So I was only here to appease my broken heart, to become a gemologist, to do the thing I worried I would never do if I did not do it now. So? Was this the worst thing?

There's a garden behind St. Luke's church that I liked to sneak away to on idle afternoons. I'd sit on a bench with a book but find myself rarely reading. The people occupying the other benches were too distracting, even by their very presence. I'd watch them and wonder what had caused each one to be at this particular garden. The boy and girl who had obviously left their places of work to meet for a quick lunch amidst roses. The older man sipping at melting ice in a plastic cup, the creases of years making him look both more fierce and inviting than he surely was. The woman with hair dyed blue, dropping obscenities into an animated phone conversation. How had they each come to be in New

York? How was it that they seemed to fit here, in this garden, in this city? And what could I do to shake the notion that if any of them glanced at me, they'd have known right away that I wasn't in it like they were; that I was not the real thing.

Looking down at the small piece of cardstock in my hands, I could see the faint remnant of lettering where my name and phone number had once been. But only at close range, and only if the sun were hitting at just the right angle. Otherwise, the cardstock looked completely blank. Otherwise, you'd have no idea anything had ever been there. Otherwise, it was as if it had never happened.

COMING

"I'M ACTUALLY KIND OF JEALOUS," MY BOSS said, after I'd told him I was moving to Manhattan. "I mean, that's not just some city. It's *New York*."

He said this in such a way that suggested he was not only impressed with my gumption but also genuinely covetous that I was at a point in life that would even allow for such a move in the first place. My boss, married with three children, most likely suffered from some amount of Suburbia burnout. Not that he didn't love his wife and family, but there were times when I wondered if he looked at himself and liked what he saw. He'd recently been dubbed the "Fat Skinny Guy"—in jest, by a few of our more charismatic colleagues—for having put on enough weight in recent years to have achieved Dad Bod status.

And I knew what they meant. Because the weight made a difference. I'd been shocked to realize shortly before this New York conversation that despite being a director at our company and having a wife and three children and strands of gray peppering the sides of his hair, he was younger than the man who'd just broken my heart. And even having cause to put your boss in the You-and-I-Could-Conceivably-Date bucket is pretty disgusting. Bottom line: the man looked older than he was. And I don't know, maybe that's just what happens to people when life cements them in, such that they can't decide one day to just up and move to New York.

Not that I'd just up and decided.

New York was what I planned to do if my boyfriend, the man who was older than my Director Boss, ever decided to cut me loose. Which he did. In epic fashion.

The thing about saying you're moving to New York, however, is that it's a lot easier than actually moving to New York. And at the top of my Moving to New York Checklist was that I would need a job. And finding a job in New York City struck me as something that might be kind of difficult. Especially a job that involved doing something I liked, that paid well, and which did not require a 2.5-hour one-way commute to Long Island.

My obvious preference was to keep my current job. Not only because this was the easiest thing, but also because my job *was* well-paying, and I *did* like it. As if this weren't enough, I cannot overstate how much I enjoyed working for this particular boss. I really did. For perhaps the first time, here was a superior that I truly got along with and was not at all annoyed by, condescended to, or embarrassed over. He was actually fun, entertained me greatly, and always found ways to make me feel fortunate to be part of his team. And really, how often in life does a girl find that? For me, it's just been the one time.

I remember when he'd been hired, initially joining the team as a product manager, quickly rising the ranks through a slew of marketing roles, and ultimately attaining a directorship of one of our specialty label departments there at Pressure-Sensitive Leader in Cleveland, Ohio. That's when I began working for him. For accuracy's sake, I must point out that one of the other people on his team—a man closer to me in age and life situation than my Director Boss—was actually the one to whom our org charts had me reporting. But it was one of those arrangements that felt insincere, like it was just for show; something they were doing to give this younger man a "development opportunity" even though he really didn't have much in the way of additional experience or strategy to offer me.

While we got along fine, this Baby Boss and me, and he certainly did help me in many aspects of my day to day job, our Director Boss was still the one who resonated with me as the person for whom I truly worked; the person who could best help me learn and grow and hone my budding skills for shaping marketing strategy; and, certainly, the one to whom I would want to confess my very real need to leave town when my boyfriend, who worked just one floor below us in the same building, left my heart in shards.

The problem with leaving town yet keeping my current job was that I didn't see how I could accomplish both. My office was in Cleveland. More than that, the headquarters of the division of our company for which I worked were in Cleveland.

So, like, *all* of our offices were in Cleveland.

Working remotely from New York was a bit of a tough sell. But that didn't stop me from running the data. I traveled a fair amount in my role, visiting various customers and sales reps, which meant there were already chunks of time that I wasn't in the office anyway. Most of these customers tended to be in the tri-state area, too. So, see, wouldn't it actually make *more* sense for me to be working out of New York?

Besides, what work can a person *not* accomplish with a computer and a cell phone? I maintain the answer to that question is none. Meaning anything that can be done while sitting in an office cubicle can certainly be done while sitting in bed or in a cushy sunroom chaise. In fact, it can probably be done better and faster because working in your pajamas is super motivating, as is the smell of blueberry muffins wafting in from the kitchen. So armed with a bit of data on how many of my days were travel days as well as the location of this travel, all that remained was to wait for the right moment to make my case to my Director Boss.

I may be a bitch for this — although at least I'm an *opportunistic* bitch — but the right moment turned out to be when I found out that my actual supervisor, my Baby Boss, was in the process of negotiating a new job halfway across the country and would be leaving the company. He hadn't told our Director Boss yet, and let me assure you that I did not out him. Nor would I have ever. I'm not *that* bitchy. But I did decide to beat him to the punch.

I told our Director Boss that continuing to remain in Cleveland was becoming a struggle for me personally, and that it was perhaps going to be necessary, sooner rather than later, for me to relocate. I told him this most likely meant New York City, and, since you'll never get what you don't ask for, brought up the travel data I'd collected and pitched the idea of me working from New York remotely. A long shot, sure, and I admitted it. But it wasn't the *worst* idea in world, and he admitted that. I think at the end of the day though, we both knew it was an argument I would never win. Regardless, when I left his office that day, my Director Boss certainly knew I was a flight risk. Mission accomplished.

How much the Director Boss really cared about this piece of information, or what, if any, action he may have taken to prevent my flight had my Baby Boss stayed put is something I suppose we'll never know, because my Baby Boss promptly turned in his resignation. A bit panicked, my Director Boss almost immediately called me into his office.

"Let's talk about New York," he said as soon as the door was closed.

And I almost felt bad. Bad that I'd put my Director Boss, this man for whom I so enjoyed working, in this predicament. My Baby Boss and I were the only two people in the whole company who managed a particular line of specialty labels. They couldn't afford to lose us both; it would be crippling. But then, I'd known that. It's precisely why I'd done what I'd done. So yeah, I felt a little bad. But mostly I felt freaking amazing, because my strategic prowess had just landed me a one-way ticket to New York.

My Director Boss and I worked out the details (me,

working remotely, from New York City), and I picked a move date six weeks out.

Honestly, I couldn't believe I'd actually pulled it off. Bring on the pajamas and the sunroom chaise. I could smell the blueberry muffins already.

GOING

WHAT DO YOU DO WHEN YOUR DAYS ARE numbered? When there's a finite, limited amount of time in which to accomplish everything you wish to in a place? How do you prioritize? Keep track? Where do you even begin?

I'll tell you what you do. You make a bucket list.

NYC Bucket List quickly became the most frequently accessed spreadsheet on my computer, its little icon saved to the desktop view, a constant reminder both of my departure and how much I wanted to do and see before I left.

I'll just tell you right now that the only thing on the list that truly left me hanging was tickets to the Jimmy Fallon show. They're so in demand that I could never get any once a new batch of tickets was released. It bugs me a little to this day, because I really tried. What's a girl gotta do, Jimmy?

All things considered—like, I don't know, the fact that it's the largest city in the country and I hadn't lived there very long—it was a pretty modest list. It was composed of both things I'd never done before and things I *had* done but wanted to do again before I left.

Sixty percent of these were what I would call attractions. Things I wanted to see. Museums, like the Queens Museum of Art or the Botanical Gardens. Parks and monuments such as the Greenwood Cemetery and the garden at Riverside Park. Some of these had always been on my list, and some had been added throughout my time in the city.

Several of these attractions were end points of various subway trains. Because there's something that happens after waiting for trains every day. There's a place your mind goes when staring at the words of the signs that announce the train line and the direction it's going. I probably stared more than most, partly because I was overly concerned with making sure I'd entered on the correct side of the street, but mostly because I wondered about these final stops, the ones used to announce where a train was ultimately headed.

Where exactly *was* Pelham Bay Park, for instance? And what was it? I would never have a reason to go there, to just be passing through that particular corner of the Bronx, so one day I rode the 6 train as far as it would go. I was the only one still in my train car once we reached Pelham Bay. It was cold, spring not yet in bloom, and I surely hadn't given the park the chance to put its best foot forward. I might have been underwhelmed regardless given Manhattan's beloved Central Park, so full of people and life, but I still put in my time. I walked around between various statues and benches and small leafless trees and felt content in the knowledge that this was Pelham Bay Park. This was where the train went. This was the end of the line.

South Ferry was another such place, one that marked the end point of the 1 line and the boarding place for the Staten Island Ferry. I'd never been to Staten Island—again, I never had a reason to go there—but I'd wondered about that ferry each time I boarded the 1 train. What was it like? Where exactly did it go? There were people who commuted every day on this very ferry, so how could I leave the city without ever having been?

It's a pretty simple process once you reach the ferry station, one full of mostly tourists on the sunny spring after-noon that I took the 1 train to its endpoint. You buy a ticket to the ferry, which leaves about every half hour. A thick mass of people board with excitement, all looking for the best views and best places to take selfies with those views in the background. I picked a sunny spot on the bottom level and leaned my face slightly out as we sped along the water, on our way to Staten Island.

Once there, I turned right around and bought a return ticket, enjoying the second leg even more as Manhattan got closer and closer. It was such a beautiful view to return to. Kind of like the sunset sail I ended up taking a few weeks before moving. It was another attraction on my list, one that takes you out on a big, old-school sailing ship just before sunset. It's light when you leave, Manhattan's downtown buildings silvery from the late afternoon sun.

As the sun disappears, however, the buildings light up against the darkening sky. Such that I couldn't decide which

I found more breathtaking. The view from way out in the water of the skyline at dusk, or the sun setting just behind the Statue of Liberty, which our ship sailed in front of at just the right moment. I felt equal parts proud and excited to call this place my home, to have lived here for any season of life, but also hesitant and somewhat guilty over having decided to leave. Because who, really, would do that? Who would leave this?

Another category on the NYC Bucket List, representing 30 percent of the items, was food. Revisiting favorites like Serendipity and Bad Horse Pizza. Trying new places like Buttermilk Bakery and Lexington Soda Shop. The soda shop was a special one and I returned multiple times, usually alone and usually for a butterscotch sundae. It's the kind of place that has made no effort to modernize or remodel. It is, to be frank, nothing to write home about, both outside and in, but it's reminiscent of the kind of place you could have found decades ago. And when bringing bite after bite of melted vanilla mixed with golden butterscotch to my mouth, I couldn't think much beyond the moment. And isn't that the point?

Before moving to Harlem—back when I lived on the Upper East Side—I read an article about a premium Thai restaurant and so had given Jaiya a try early on. It's going to sound like hyperbole, but their Pad Thai is the best I've ever tasted, so the bucket list portion of this was going back to Jaiya as many times as I could before leaving. I'd suggest it when meeting almost anyone for lunch, and once when a friend more budget conscious than I was suggested that we *split* an order of the Pad Thai (which was over $20 with tax and tip), my heart sank. I can still remember how forlornly I looked at the little half portion sitting on my plate.

The remaining 10 percent of items on the list were shows. Seeing *Les Miserables* on Broadway, which I'd always wanted to do, or seeing *The Curious Incident of the Dog in the Nighttime*, which made me cry a kind of helpless, inspired cry that feels equal parts triumphant and sad. The wildcard was the Rockettes, which I had in my head as this thing that I needed to see before I left. Not that I could understand why. A bunch of super fit women wearing lots of makeup and kicking their legs? *That's* what I couldn't do without?

But I'm telling you right now that there's something about sitting in Radio City Music Hall watching these women do what they do. There's something about the perfection they achieve together that created one of my fondest New York City memories. I'll never understand it in a way that makes me feel like the cultured feminist that I am, but I guess that's the thing about New York. You never know what will stick.

And that's what I think when I look over my NYC Bucket List today. How I had high hopes for some things that ended up leaving me underwhelmed or feeling annoyed that I'd ventured so far to see them. Others seemed silly or second string and were among my very favorite experiences. So on any given day in New York, you have to be willing to let go of the way you thought it would be, the way you wanted it to be.

The simplest way I can put it is there are things that living in New York City leaves on you. Things you can't shake. Like how luxurious toasters, dishwashers, and garbage disposals have seemed to me ever since. How delightful to pull out the toaster that you have counter space for and simply pop a piece of bread in. How convenient to not have to wash your lone plate and set of silverware by hand after every meal. How handy to own more than one plate, spoon, knife, and fork in the first place.

I can't shake the freedom of having access to such a vast and vibrant city, or how much I miss that. Because by leaving, you give up the ability to watch the sunrise on the Brooklyn Bridge. Or catch the off-Broadway play that your friend is stage managing. Or go to Serendipity just because you feel like it. Or explore Central Park in every season. And these are not little things. These are things that make nearly every aspect of the sleepy little beach town you move away to seem utterly unremarkable.

Mostly I can't shake the shame of having chosen the sleepy little beach town. Of preferring it, even when fully aware of what I've left behind. Of waking up every morning knowing that leaving was the right decision. There's a shame in that. One that comes over me with every ocean sunset. Because I eat at my little town's few restaurants over and over again. I walk the same village streets. My days are far less varied than they were in New York, and is that *better*?

On my most epic day in New York, I set out to hit ten things I'd wanted to do, a combination of new things and favorites:

1. A beautiful sunny day, my first stop was Dominique Ansel's Bakery in Soho for a cronut, a place I ventured to once a month to try his newest, never-repeating flavor.

2. Next on the list was Pippin Vintage Jewelry, a store I'd read about as having the best vintage collection available in the city. I came away without having bought anything, but only barely.

3. Chelsea Market was next, a delightful collection of vendors in a warm and inviting space that I visited often, my favorite thing being the rosemary potatoes at Dickson's Farmstand Meats.

4. The High Line is an elevated park built on an old railway line, a skinny thing that stretches over downtown. I had it on my list that day and spent some time waxing pensive while looking out into Chelsea Harbor.

5. The Central Park Carousel was next, a fixture I had tried to find a few times before but had always somehow gotten lost (it's a big park, okay?). On this day I found it, waited in line as the only childless adult, and felt positively buoyant as my horse bobbed up and down, lush greenery rolling by in the background.

6. Tiffany's was a must, the 1.63 carat diamond necklace I tried on that day being one of the most spectacular pieces I'd ever had the guts to ask to see outside the case.

7. Reading outside was on my list that day, which
    I did on a bench in the sunshine, pausing
    every few moments to watch other New
    Yorkers eat their lunch at small tables or walk
    in laughing pairs down the street.

8. And for all my reading and checking out of
    books while living in New York, the proximity
    of local branches made it relatively easy to
    have avoided the New York Public Library's
    flagship location with its famous lions guarding
    the entrance. So this day marked the first
    time I had ever gone inside this spectacular
    building, sighing over the cavernous space and
    beautiful ceilings.

9. Most of my time in Manhattan was spent
    living on its easternmost edge, which meant
    that an imperceptible symmetry seemed mine
    for the taking if I only visit Riverside Park, the
    westernmost edge of the island. On this epic
    day I did that, just as darkness was winning its
    daily battle and the view across the water made
    me feel so very *west*.

10. Frozen Hot Chocolate at Serendipity closed
    out the day, a group of friends meeting me
    there for what was a perfect final stop.

But see, that's what I'm talking about. Days like this are what you can't do when you live anywhere else. Nowadays, with a free day in Southern California, I spend it reading, tinkering with whatever manuscript I'm in the middle of, and strolling along the beach as the sun dips down along the horizon.

As to which of those two kinds of days I like better? I'd rather not answer.

COMING

WHEN I MOVED TO CLEVELAND AFTER FINISHING
graduate school, it was the first time I'd ever had my own
place. I'd been living a truly student life in a furnished
house with two roommates, and I really didn't own anything.
Nothing. But this is not so much the story of how I used
my signing bonus from Pressure-Sensitive Leader to furnish
my first home and proceeded to spend the next seven years
accumulating possessions as it is the story of how I had to
then whittle those possessions and furnishings down to what
would fit inside a 350-square-foot apartment.

That's all I had to work with in the Manhattan lease I'd
just signed. Three hundred and fifty square feet. Just think
about that for a moment. Think about fitting everything you
own into one room. Think about getting rid of everything

else, despite the money you spent or the memories created by each item's acquisition.

I realized I had a problem when I tackled the first thing on my list, the clothes closet, and only ended up with a couple of items I was willing to part with. I mean, I shopped at Anthropologie, for crying out loud. Clearly this was going to be tougher than I thought, so I turned to a book called *The Joy of Less*. I confess I didn't read the whole thing, both because each chapter was a rehashing of the book's main point (life is simpler and better with less), and because I didn't need a tutorial on how to decide what to keep (do you actually use it?). I just needed to pull the trigger on actually answering that question.

The dress I wore to a friend's brother's wedding:

> Have you worn it since?
> *No.*
> Then get rid of it.
> *But look at the cute little gold circles on it.*
> That's a stupid thing to bring up.
> *You're kind of mean.*
> Then look at it this way. Is the fabric kind of itchy anyway?
> *Yes.*
> I win.
> *You're still mean.*

The KitchenAid Stand Mixer I got during an internship at Well-Known Appliances Conglomerate:

> How often do you use it?
> *Once a year to make cheesecake for*
> *Thanksgiving.*
> Then get rid of it.
> *But what will I do at Thanksgiving?*
> Beat the batter by hand.
> *That sounds really hard. Plus I'm sure I'll use it*
> *more if I keep it.*
> In New York? With twelve inches of counter
> space?
> *Then I guess I won't need the springform pans*
> *either.*
> That's my girl.
> *That sounds gross. Who even are you?*
> I am logic. I am what you know you should do.
> *I think I'm hallucinating.*

The two-part reading chaise that ended up being the most expensive piece of furniture in my house because I thought the price was for both sections instead of just one, and by the time the store called to tell me about the misunderstanding, I was too embarrassed to cancel the order so I had them deliver it anyway:

> How often do you sit in it?
> *I sit in it.*

How often?
That's not important.
It's the only thing that's important.
I rarely sit in it.
Then get rid of it.
But I spent all that money.
You don't sit in it.
It's for reading.
Is that where you read?
Sometimes. Rarely.
That's the second time you've used that word.
I hate you.
You hate me because I'm right.
Well I still hate you.

And on and on. Perhaps tough at first, but what surprised me most about this downsizing process was that once I bought into the idea that only my most favorite, most used possessions were worth keeping, it was shockingly easy to get rid of almost everything I owned. I could look at something and immediately deduce it didn't make sense to keep it; that there was no reason to have it take up any of my 350 square feet in New York.

Surely the author of *The Joy of Less*, not to mention the bitchy voice of logic in my head, would have been proud to see my driveway and front yard so full during my pre-move sale. It was a week before I moved, and from clothes to shoes to books to movies to furniture, there it all sat. Waiting to be purchased.

And even though at that point I'd already come to grips

with the need to get rid of so much, it's a strange thing to actually see it piled in front of you. To see people perusing it, touching it, haggling with you to charge less for it. Even in my minimalist resoluteness, there were moments when the yard sale itself shook my resolve.

Am I really doing this? Am I moving to New York? Is this whole thing the worst idea I've ever had? At the very least, is it a mistake? At this point, could I get out of it if I wanted to? Could I tell that man to unhand my breakfast table; that woman to stop picking through my stemware? Or to at least take the whole effing set so she doesn't leave me with pieces I can't sell? Bitch.

For Christmas during one of my teen years, what I wanted most was the show *24* on DVD. Miraculously, I ended up with seasons one and two, each gloriously bound in their own boxed set. For more years than they should have, these sets meant a great deal to me. Not just because those first couple of *24* seasons were so good, but also because they represented something that didn't often happen in my childhood: getting what I wanted. Or, more to the point, getting what I wanted when what I wanted cost more than, say, a new pair of Payless shoes. I'm exaggerating, but it's true that Christmas gifts in the Nay home were always of a modest variety, and so my two boxed sets were that much more precious. Maybe my siblings had gotten a little less because of me; maybe my parents had sacrificed a little more.

And so amidst the sea of strangers walking off with my belongings, the wave that undid me was the man trying to haggle with me for my two *24* seasons. I was parting with them because I was parting with everything, and while I thought $10 per season was more than fair even at garage sale standard, he only wanted to pay $5 per season.

I refused.

The man persisted, coming back the next day with the same offer.

Again I refused, but he hung around.

"You want to get rid of them, don't you?" he asked.

I did.

"And wouldn't you rather they go to someone who's a true fan?"

I would.

But they were so expensive. My parents. Christmas. The Counter Terrorism Unit. All those discs.

And suddenly the refrain of *The Joy of Less*—the reality that I hadn't even watched a single episode in easily a decade—was battling the specialness of what was such a pivotal childhood moment. They had *meant* something to me. They didn't anymore. So how does that net out?

I watched the man walk away with the two boxed sets under his arm, his $5 bills feeling dirty in my hands, but wasn't this the point? Shouldn't I have been happy to have found a buyer? I remember making $1,500 from that sale, which seems incredibly successful for your run-of-the-mill yard sale in the Midwest. But given it represented almost everything I owned, it felt overwhelmingly like a loss.

Maybe I should have kept the DVDs.

I'm sorry, Jack.

Sidebar: Peeing at Tiffany's and New York City's Biggest Problem

New York City has a lot going for it. It's part of the reason why I never became particularly enthused about rooting for any of their sports teams. Unlike Cleveland, a blue collar town that has literally *nothing* going for it except the fans who pile into the stadiums year after year, New York simply doesn't need that kind of help or devotion. It doesn't need

stadiums packed with fans gathered to fight for just a single win or to celebrate the awesomeness that is New York. It doesn't need championships to validate its success. New York *is* a success.

You could say it's because New York is a cultural mecca, offering exposure to such rich collections of art and history. Or perhaps it's the diversity, the melting pot that brings so many nationalities to the same neighborhood streets. The public transit system is vast, and, relatively speaking, a pretty cheap way to get around. It's the worldwide capital of musical theater, and you can have your pick of global cuisines delivered to your door at any time of day or night. Even the very network that keeps the eight million of us flushing toilets, drinking water, heating apartments, and flipping light switches is a downright world wonder. I've done some research on the infrastructure of New York City, and it's simply unparalleled. Take trash removal alone.

I could go on, but I trust you're with me when I say New York is a desirable place. It's fortunate. It doesn't need your love or loyalty.

But there is one area where New York City falls desperately short. It's something that really ought to factor into relocation decisions, and that is the total lack of public restroom access. You think I'm exaggerating for effect, but I promise I'm not. Needing a bathroom while out and about is going to be something that happens to you.

It first happened to me a couple of weeks after I'd moved in. With some friends on a walking tour of Wall Street, we ended the outing with a stop at a small bagel shop and I began to be aware of a feminine situation that needed to be addressed. The shop didn't have a restroom, so I bade farewell to my friends, feigning a need to get home.

If life has taught me anything about restrooms, it's that you can always count on Starbucks, so I didn't immediately panic. I simply Googled the nearest Starbucks. But apparently not all Starbucks locations *have* restrooms, a fact I hadn't known until that day on Wall Street, and by this time, my feminine situation was quickly escalating to an emergency.

Let me pause to just clarify that when I say emergency, I'm talking about blood. *Blood*, people. Including but not limited to: blood on me, blood on my clothes, blood visible to the world in a very embarrassing way. Welcome to the life of a menstruating woman.

My next thought was of Tiffany & Co., because one of the best things about their flagship store is that it has a restroom—a very fancy one at that—available for customer use. I was nowhere near the flagship store, but perhaps this meant that *all* Tiffany locations had restrooms. Didn't that stand to reason? Weren't rich people spending tons of time in there whilst deciding between enormous solitaires? Didn't these rich people need convenient locations in which to pee between seeing the round brilliant and oval shaped options?

Swinging open the door of the Wall Street Tiffany location with purpose, I was soon informed that, no, Tiffany locations do *not* all have restrooms. So if you're a rich person wanting to spend tons of time deciding between solitaires while being served blue box-shaped bonbons and champagne and then have the ability to use the restroom should your feminine backup fail, you'll pretty much have to go to the flagship store. Words to live by, people.

By now I was in bad shape, standing still on the sidewalk with absolutely no idea how to get myself to a restroom. I could have cried if the whole thing didn't feel so much like an episode of a sitcom.

The One With the Tampon Fail.

Finally a thought occurred to me, the memory of having joined a gym a few days prior. New York Sports Club is nothing to write home about, and I hated paying the hefty membership fee—I was pretty sure I was being exploited* just because I'd joined at the location next to my apartment

---

*When I moved to Harlem the following year, I couldn't help but notice the cost for new members to join was much lower.

on the Upper East Side—but in my bloody state of clarity, I saw my contract not so much as a gym membership, but as access to restrooms in over fifty locations throughout the city's boroughs.

Eureka!

I walked as quickly as I could to the nearest New York Sports Club location, only a few blocks away. The woman who scanned my membership card might have thought it strange that I had nothing with me with which to work out— no gear, no clothes, no shoes or bag, not even a purse—or that I exited out the same door less than five minutes later, but that's not really the point. The point is that I had discovered the secret to public restroom access in New York City.

I used this trick countless times over the course of my tenure in New York, and it was such a comfort to know there was almost always somewhere close by where I could go should the need arise. It's the best advice I can give to anyone living in or moving to the city. Get a gym membership. I'm serious. Even if you never work out once, it will be the best city money you ever spend. Especially if you're a girl.

GOING

WHEN MY AUNT LEAH CAME TO VISIT ME IN
New York, the timing coincided perfectly with an upcoming
job interview.

Changing careers had been on my mind since before I'd
even moved to New York, as I'd long had gemology on the
brain. And this particular interview was for a position in the
marketing department at the world's largest gem institute. It
aligned very nicely with my interests and past experience,
and in many ways I considered it a dream job.

While still in Cleveland, I'd hired a life coach to help
me sort through how exactly I would go about switching
careers. At the time it seemed a rather Herculean task. I had
no connections within the gem and jewelry industry, having
gone a completely different way with my career.

Through a series of exercises and assignments, my life coach had me pinpoint where exactly within this new industry I wanted to be, and also mapped out a series of steps she recommended to help me get there. I started leveraging LinkedIn, and through a connection with a business school classmate, I ended up in touch with a marketing vice president at the gem institute. I registered for an upcoming gem and jewelry career fair in Manhattan, and I asked the marketing VP if there was to be anyone in attendance that she'd recommend I meet. The VP wasn't going to be at the career fair, but she gave me the name of her boss, who *would* be there, and I wrote it down in my notebook, circling it several times.

I didn't realize until I was sitting through the career fair's opening panel at the Javits Center that the name I'd written down was that of the gem institute's chief marketing officer. Nor did I realize that she was in charge of the entire event. The personification of Head Honcho, this petite woman in her sixties was as classy as they come, a downright force both within the gem industry and her own organization.

It's not so much that my heart sank, it's more that it was seized by panic. Because how could I introduce myself to this woman? Where would I even find the opportunity? She was literally running the show.

While walking around the fair later that afternoon, a crisp stack of resumes in hand, I caught a glimpse of her, alone and walking in the opposite direction. This was my chance, yet I must have turned around half a dozen times, losing my nerve about the wisdom of approaching such an important woman with the very menial topic of my future employment.

But this was it. This was what I had. It was why I had

come here. And some chances you don't get a second time. So I turned back around, quickened my pace, and spoke her name. She stopped and turned around, a look of skepticism and annoyance on her face.

What happened next though was remarkable, because as I introduced myself and explained my connection to her employee, the VP, as well as my background in marketing and my career ambitions within the gem industry, I could tell she was impressed. Her entire demeanor changed, and our impromptu conversation in the middle of the busy aisle went on much longer than I'd expected it to. I left her with a resume, and she invited me to meet with her when I went to California the following month for a gemology class, which I did.

Over many months, I kept in touch with both the VP and the chief marketing officer, and while they did speak of a position they were looking to create within their marketing department that would be a great fit for me, it wasn't ready yet, and I couldn't put all my eggs in this one basket when it came to looking for employment. Plus, they'd been clear about their organization's general policy, which was that they only hired locally.

Yet there I was the following spring, preparing to complete my gemology diploma in a matter of weeks and the gem institute's new marketing position ready and posted. The timing was perfect, and somehow I'd convinced them to fly me in from New York to interview, even though they had a fresh crop of California girls ready to be hired.

So clearly I needed a new outfit.

Enter Aunt Leah, who arrived on the morning redeye and spent most of the day marching me up and down Fifth

Avenue. Leah's always good for a project, but a *shopping* project? She was in her element, and I was in the world's most capable hands for such a task. She didn't even live here, yet she knew the locations of all the stores. She knew just where we had seen that blouse I liked best. She knew how to maximize sales and points to find the best deals.

We settled on a black skirt suit from Banana Republic, with a sheer, bee-patterned black and white blouse from Ann Taylor. For shoes I wanted a fresh pop of color. Leah identified coral as the winning ticket and proceeded to gather the best candidates from the shoe department at Lord & Taylor. She had half a dozen or so rounded up, the finalists, and I tried them each on, a bit internally panicked over how much this single outfit was costing me. Especially when my favorite pair—a Kenneth Cole heel in a bold poppy color that cut across the foot leaving the inner part sexily uncovered—was the most expensive option. After all, I'd quit my job to study gemology so I wasn't working. And what if I spent all this money and then didn't get the job? I mentioned this to Leah, but she didn't seem worried.

"These shoes are going to get you that job," she said as we both looked at me in the department store mirror.

And maybe they did. Two of my interviewers specifically mentioned the shoes—the chief marketing officer, whom I'd already met, and a handsome salesman in his mid-forties who would later tell me I had a knack for color combinations.* And at my first staff meeting, the chief marketing

---

*He would also later tell me, in a note that accompanied a bottle of Chanel No. 5, that it was time to start smelling like a woman. As opposed to what, I'm really not sure.

officer introduced me by telling the story of our meeting at the career fair in New York.

She told it much differently than I remembered, that of a young woman who with confidence and poise articulated what she wanted and then made it happen. The version in my memory is more like me, an idiot, shaking in my boots, but perhaps that just goes to show that bravery has a longer shelf-life than fear.

"Let that be a lesson to us all," she continued in front of a boardroom full of our entire marketing team. "She knew what she wanted and she went out and she got it."

I blushed a little at the attention and looked down to see that I was wearing the poppy shoes, so of course I thought of Leah, who hadn't sounded the least bit surprised when I told her I'd gotten the job. Then again, she'd already called it.

These shoes are going to get you that job.

And to think I'd almost bought a cheaper pair.

Coming

THE FIRST THING I NOTICED ABOUT MY APART~
ment when I moved in was that it smelled funny. A smell
that hadn't been there when I'd come to the open house a
month earlier and fallen in love with the place. I initially
dismissed this move-in day smell as something in the realm
of cleaning; of changing ownership; of whatever my landlord and her husband had done to get the place ready for
my arrival.

Besides, I had a lot on my mind that afternoon. There
really wasn't room for any nonsense or bitching about what
I may or may not have *smelled* in the apartment. Only
moments before I'd stepped out of a taxi onto my new
Manhattan street. I'd stood in front of the bright red door
and looked up at my building, three suitcases and a cat in

tow. I'd walked by the mailboxes in the entryway and seen my name already written on a small white placard above the box for 3C. And I'd walked the two flights up to my door and entered the threshold of my apartment for the first time since being its occupant.

I was a New Yorker.

As in, I lived here. I would return here after trips. People would send me mail and it would come here.

So did it really matter that my apartment smelled weird?

The answer to that question may have been *no* had it not continued to bother me as the afternoon wore on. I unpacked, aware that the familiarity of the smell was kicking in. So was an acute headache. It was a gas smell. Or was at least in the gas family. To the point where I began to wonder if there was really anything keeping my new apartment from exploding.

This had been a fear of mine prior to the move. Gas. And having to cook with it. An open flame and the consequent chance for things to go horribly awry had been overly concerning to me ever since my mid-twenties, when I had an accident with fire.

Even the *idea* of gas and flame in my new apartment made me check the fire escape plan (basically stare out the window at the escape hatch) so often that I really should have talked to a therapist about it. And this was more than just the *idea* of it. This was *reality*. Gas. And flame. In my apartment.

I broke down and mentioned the smell to my landlord, who explained that it was indeed coming from the small range in my kitchen. It was one of those ranges that had a pilot light in its inner workings that was always on. And it was particularly pungent that day, as the pilot light had just been re-lit after sitting dormant through the previous tenant's lease. She'd opted to simply not use the oven.

Let's just think about this for a moment.

The only other kitchen appliance present was a tiny microwave. Meaning my predecessor had subsisted on a diet composed entirely of either takeout or whatever could be cooked in a microwave. This struck me as very sad. And kind of disgusting. And while it didn't take too long before I'd been sucked into shockingly similar habits myself, on move-in day, I very much wanted the use of an oven and range. I *cooked*, dammit. But if this meant the apartment always smelling this arrestingly gassy way, I wasn't sure I could handle it.

My landlord proposed shutting off the pilot light and having me light it only when I wanted to cook. At least that way my apartment wasn't sitting in this vat of gassiness 24-7. Which would have been a perfectly reasonable solution had lighting the pilot involved an on/off switch. Instead I watched my landlord demonstrate by turning on the gas valve, getting on her hands and knees, and blindly reaching up from the ground into the inner workings of the oven with a lighter.

Oh, *hell* no.*

There was simply no way I was going to do this. Even one time. Let alone every time I wanted to so much as scramble an egg. Even if I *could* manage to not burn down the building, the stress of whether or not I *would* burn down the building is something with which I would always wrestle. Sure, you can boil this all down to a very real need

---

*And if people are saying *yes* to this, honestly, why are more apartments in New York City not blowing up? This is a serious question that I would like answered.

for therapy, or you can boil it down to the even more real need to cook without having to physically *light* anything. I mean, am I reaching for the stars on this, people?

And so I resorted to a hot plate my landlord provided, opting to leave the gassy pilot light off. And while this meant scrambling eggs took longer than usual, left me completely without the use of an oven, and subjected me to the occasional concerned comment from friends and family about the fact that I was a grown woman who was perhaps at a point in life where cooking with a hot plate was no longer really okay, it was still better than the gas.

I was also perhaps at a point in life where lighting a pilot light shouldn't freak me out, but nobody's perfect.

Sidebar: Public Transportation and New York City's Quietest Night

I didn't have a car while living in New York, which suited me just fine. I'd had to pay a hefty cancellation fee to get out of the lease I was in the middle of at the time of my move, but there was never any question in my mind. Absolutely no part of me felt compelled to drive myself around Manhattan.*

What was so mind-boggling as I walked through the city was how many people had cars. I figured these were the types who disliked relinquishing control, who preferred to be behind the wheel of their own commutes, who wanted to avoid the frequent disruptions that plagued the Manhattan transportation system, remarkable as it was. Also, I figured, these were all the rich people. Those who could afford not only a car payment but also a monthly parking or storage fee at both their apartment and office buildings.

People who drove cars also had to pay for car insurance and gasoline,

---

*I became so used to not driving that when moving to California—I rented a car and drove cross-country—I was convinced that the muscle weakness I felt in my hands was the start of some horrible degenerative disease. It turned out to *not* be a degenerative disease, rather that I was simply no longer used to gripping a steering wheel for five days straight. A mix-up that could happen to anyone.

other costs I no longer had. Really the only cost to public transportation in New York is a person's metro card, which can be purchased based on time, say, unlimited use for a month, or money, say, $20, after which you'll need to refill with more money. Obviously, the puzzle of which makes more financial sense depends on how much you actually use the public transportation system.

Depending on what I had scheduled for a particular week, sometimes I'd put money on the card and try to make it last as long as I could, maybe turning down a few social engagements and activities, or walking more instead of taking the subway or bus. I never cared much for the money method, in that it affected my choices and how free I felt to explore the city, to say yes when invited out. Going with the time method and splurging on an unlimited card afforded me what felt like complete luxury. It inspired me to get out more, to purposely explore new places and boroughs, to choose "go" when the question was whether to go or stay, to swipe in the downtrodden hanging around the turnstiles asking passersby to help them out. And given the at-the-time cost of $110 for a 30-day unlimited ride card, if you planned on more than one subway ride per day, it made better financial sense anyway.

Aside from eliminating the cost and stress, the biggest benefit to not having a car in New York is the amount of time you spend walking. Walking to the subway, the library, the grocery store, the gym, the hair salon, the doctor, the bakery, the diner, the theater. Ask yourself right now, from your house and two-car-garage in suburbia, when was the last time you walked to *any* of these places or appointments?

How about *all* of them? From the increase in physical activity to the increase, equally rewarding, in the things you see and notice in your own surroundings, the change to the walking life is nothing short of delightful.

While visiting Manhattan recently for a work trip, I challenged myself to walk everywhere instead of take the subway and was reminded of both of these benefits—the physical and the observatory. One morning I woke up early to get a cronut from Dominique Ansel's bakery on Spring Street, a 2.5-mile walk from my hotel. By the time I showed up for work that morning, I'd already taken 12,000 steps. I'd already walked past the Flatiron building, through Washington Square Park, and looked up at the Empire State Building as the morning sun glistened off its windows. Who of my colleagues could say *that*, each showing up in a cab, looking tired and rushed with their Starbucks cups in hand?

Another significant benefit to not driving is you don't have to worry about inclement weather in the same way you used to. A commute into my East Cleveland office could take triple its normal time on snowy days. And there are things beyond the weather itself that you can't control in those situations—like other drivers. Like other *stupid* drivers. I came to dread any sign of snow, especially on a weekday, and I'm convinced the hours I spent sliding and skidding over icy roads just trying to get home have taken years off my life.

In New York, snow was simply snow. I might put on boots and a hat, but it didn't really keep me from anything. I didn't have to wield a 5000-pound automobile, so nothing about it stressed me out. What's more, I was able to finally appreciate snow for what it really was, which is beautiful. It was something people actually *looked forward to*, which was a completely novel concept to me.

One afternoon during my first winter in New York, I was waiting in line at my favorite Upper East Side bakery to pick up a pie, my contribution to a Thanksgiving dinner with friends. It was a nice bakery and the pie was expensive, part of me second-guessing my choice, in that there were surely many other cheaper options I could have chosen. Like canned cranberry sauce. But these were my first holidays in the city, and I wanted to do them right. Instead of a clam-shelled cookie-cutter pie from the bread section of the corner grocer, I wanted to hold an expertly-boxed pie bound with string out to the hostess when she opened the door.

The bakery was overcrowded that day, most people getting impatient from waiting for their pumpkin or apple, everyone growing warm from the layers they had needed outside on this chilly late fall day. And just then, me wishing I were spending less money on pie and a roomful of others wishing this errand weren't taking so long, it started to snow. The first snow of the season.

To my surprise, the whole bakery, moments before acting irritable and impatient, erupted in cheers. It was a moment so disarmingly charming that I had to reorient myself as to where I was and if I were, in fact, actually asleep. Because, *snow? Seriously?* It was *snow* garnering such a unanimous and euphoric reaction. It was *snow* signaling that the holidays were really here. It was *snow* not upsetting anyone about how their drives to various dinner parties that evening would now be much more complicated. It was *snow*, and it was, for the first time in my adult life, magical.

Snow coats the city in a sort of silence, even though there are only nominally fewer cars and taxis out in inclement weather. I can remember once when this silence was exacerbated by a city-wide curfew implemented one night in advance of what was forecasted to be a historic storm. They had named the storm Juno, and by 10 p.m. on a January night, all Manhattanites were supposed to be off the roads and in their houses. Schools had already announced closures for the next day. Public transportation had already shut down.

Juno didn't end up materializing the way she was supposed to, a bit disappointing after all the hype, but I'll never forget the silence of that night, when everyone was ordered indoors. I remember lying in my bed, the window propped open, and hearing absolutely nothing outside. No cars honking, no sirens wailing, no people shouting. All that remained to be heard was the softly-falling snow. On that night, and probably every night since if I'm being honest, I thought it was the most beautiful thing I'd never heard.

GOING

I LEFT MANHATTAN WITH A DIAMOND, BUT it's not what you think.

Passing the big gemology test at the end of my studies left me feeling like I deserved a treat, something special for my efforts and success. The natural choice was jewelry, but rather surprisingly, that wasn't my first thought. My first thought was ice cream. That famous sundae at Serendipity that involved ingredients flown in from around the world and cost a whopping $1,000. It's the sundae my friend Molly and I had always planned to get if ever either of us accomplished something truly epic.

In many ways, fulfilling this gemology dream fit the bill. And while I couldn't think of anything I'd accomplish in my remaining years of life that would be as important to me — or at least as hard-won—I still couldn't shake the notion that spending $1,000 on one serving of ice cream was irresponsible. I was, after all, a regular person. True that I'd been so frugal with my savings while in New York that a good portion of them still sat in my bank account, but I wasn't one of those lucky few rich people for whom money is no object. To me, money was very much an object. And if I was going to spend $1,000 on a treat, I wanted it to be one that would last forever.

So, jewelry it was.

I started my search at Aaron Faber, having met the man himself at a gemology dinner in midtown Manhattan. He sat at my table and seemed impressed during our introduction when I mentioned my background and the desired career transition I hoped to bring about with my gemology diploma. He gave me his card and invited me to stop in and see him at the store, which I interpreted to mean that he was considering me for a job. Or that at least he was *considering* considering me. The dinner had been a letdown, one that had cost me $50 and didn't turn out to have a vegetarian option. Starving and insistent that I should be fed after having shelled out the prepaid ticket price, I stubbornly ate a few bites of the chicken breast on my plate. I then felt ashamed and slightly sickened, leaving with nothing but the hope that having attended the dinner might actually land me a job at Aaron Faber.

Inside his store the following week, I looked around at all the vintage pieces before working up the nerve to approach the counter. I knew right away that a vintage piece was what I wanted. Something with a story, a prior life, even if I knew nothing about what or where that prior life might have been. When told at the counter that Aaron was not in, I left a message with my contact information and looked through a few more cases on the way out.

The scenario repeated two or three more times, me always hoping Aaron was in (he wasn't) or that he would call me back (he didn't), and always casing the joint for a special piece I might want to buy. I never found it, the perfect piece, or maybe it's just that the whole Aaron Faber thing had left a bad taste in my mouth, and so I moved on.

Known as the king of vintage jewelry in Manhattan, Pippin Vintage Jewelry is located near Chelsea. Once I discovered it, I'd often couple a stop to look for baubles with a morning or afternoon at Chelsea Market, as they were within easy walking distance. Pippin is small, as so many Manhattan stores are, and it's full of both costume and fine pieces. The costume pieces aren't behind lock and key, their various globs of color displayed on a collection of dressers, desks, and shelves throughout the store. The long counter across the right side houses the fine pieces, those with diamonds and other precious gems.

The rings stood out to me immediately, and when it came to gems of considerable size and expense, a *diamond* ring was the only thing I'd ever really entertained owning or purchasing. It's my birthstone, my favorite gem, and the thought of my owning one being dependent on a man seemed a little ridiculous. Didn't I deserve one regardless? Wouldn't it be almost tragic to never have a diamond ring simply because no man ever decided to buy me one?

I tried on several, acting like they were all in the running, even though I knew the emerald-cut circa 1950 was the one

I would choose. Set in white gold, the diamond was actually relatively small—less than half a carat. But the sheet of white gold on which it sat extended beyond the edges of the diamond, such that it gave the illusion of a larger diamond. Picture a rectangle inside a slightly larger rectangle, and picture moving the rectangles and not being able to tell that there are actually two rectangles. Picture it all just looking like the larger rectangle. Honestly, I'd never seen a ring like this, and now that I had, I couldn't figure out why jewelry designers weren't still using the tactic. I mean, who *wouldn't* want their diamond to look bigger than it was?

Our first stop, the ring and I, was to Tiffany's Fifth Avenue store. I waited in a queue to see about having the ring sized, not realizing until a sharply-dressed man of about thirty had me in a little consultation office that Tiffany only sizes rings purchased at Tiffany.

"And where did you purchase it?" the man asked, holding my new ring by the shank and eyeing it rather critically.

"Pippin," I said confidently, happily.

"Pippin," he repeated, still looking at the ring, likely trying to decide how to break the news that I was out of luck.

The whole thing embarrassed me, mostly that I hadn't known about the rule, or at least figured it. Then the embarrassment led to anger that anyone dared take away even a portion of the diamond-owning high I had a right to be feeling. The high was restored when I, back at Aaron Faber, handed the ring over to a smiling female employee who filled out the intake ticket.

"Congratulations!" she said as soon as she saw the ring I'd brought in to be sized.

Finally, here was someone who recognized this for what it was.

"Thank you!" I replied, the intensity of my beam almost matching hers, both of us so caught up in celebrating the happy that it didn't immediately occur to me that she thought I'd gotten engaged. To me, 'congratulations' still totally applied in this situation. I'd passed my test. I was a gemologist. So I'd taken the compliment in stride. *Of course* people were congratulating me. Why shouldn't they?

In hindsight, I probably should have just lied.

"Is that the hand you're going to wear it on?" the girl asked, clearly surprised, when I held out my right hand to be measured instead of my left.

"Oh, I'm not engaged," I said.

"Oh, sorry," the girl said, her smile disappearing.

"No, I mean, it's still very much a happy thing, a congratulations thing, just not that."

This only confused her, and I flushed a deep red over the whole scene I now seemed to be causing. Not that any of this mattered. Because I had a diamond. It's silly and slightly materialistic, but I just love them. And I can't express to you how much my diamond meant to me. That I'd bought it. That I'd earned it. That I could look at this beautiful thing that grew in the earth billions of years ago and was now on my right ring finger every day.

The ring would be stolen two years later, fittingly while I was on a plane bound for JFK. Someone snatched my carry-on from the overhead bin when we landed, such that when I went to exit the plane, my suitcase wasn't there. It was the one day I hadn't worn the ring, the one day I'd simply tossed the box into my suitcase, knowing it would be right above me on the plane. There were perhaps bigger things to worry about—like how I was going to work a week-long trade show without so much as a change of underwear—but all I cared about was that ring. I cried immediately, despite the airline's assurance that it was a mistake, that the suitcase would turn up. I knew it was gone.

It's just stuff, I realize, but I do wonder sometimes who has the ring now. The asshole who stole it? Some enthusiast like me who bought it at a pawn or vintage shop? A new bride just married to the thieving asshole who stole it? Whoever it is, what I would wish most of all is that they could know my story, that how the ring came to be mine and what it meant to me could be etched onto one of its facets, forever a part of its history.

I took the insurance money and had a ring designed to look like the one that had been stolen, the same sheet of white gold beneath a (bigger) emerald-cut diamond. It's not the same though. I don't like it as much. Because no matter how hard you try, you just can't make a circa 2017 look like a circa 1950. It sparkles something fantastic, but I can't help but feel sad that there's no story behind it.

Or maybe the story is that a girl had it designed to replace the vintage sparkler she bought herself after fulfilling her lifelong dream of becoming a gemologist. Maybe that's the story. And maybe it's a really good one.

COMING

ONCE I HAD SETTLED INTO MY UPPER EAST SIDE apartment, I began exploring the neighborhood. But that begged the question, just what exactly *was* my neighborhood? What constituted a neighborhood in Manhattan—a place devoid of cul-de-sacs and basketball hoops and mail boxes and tree houses? Without driveways and porches and other features that clearly delineated one's presence in a neighborhood, how did he know if he were in one? Or where one ended and the next began?

If you haven't spent much time walking around the streets of Manhattan, you might not know how frequently residential and business sectors meet. There are people living in the floors above most ground floor businesses, almost completely blurring the line between the two areas.

There's really nothing that designates a street as residential, except for maybe an overabundance of quiet and a lack of bacon wafting through the air.

As I explored my own street, a combination of residential and commercial buildings, I began to notice the core establishments that kept the residents fully functional. I list them here in no particular order:

Grocery Store

My neighborhood grocery store had a friendly, Italian-sounding name and aisles so small that you learned to resent the fools who insisted on maneuvering one of the tiny shopping carts through them. The whole interior, really, was surprisingly small. It was the kind of place that feels crowded at any time of day even with a relatively modest number of customers. I went once a week to buy staples like cat food and tortilla chips, carrying a paper bag in each hand as I walked the short distance home.

Laundromat

At first I thought I'd discovered the secret of the universe; being forced to sit while your clothes were washed and dried gave a person a series of recurring large chunks of uninterrupted reading time. But I soon got bored with waiting around while increasingly odd characters came in and out of the laundromat, so I began leaving my clothes unattended during each cycle. New Yorker friends of mine looked at me in horror when I mentioned this. I guess partly because it's a bit of a faux pas to take up a machine even a moment longer than you have to (and I was *always* late in coming back for my clothes) and partly because it's also a bit of a theft risk. Luckily I never had anything stolen or even moved, and aside from the annoyance of schlepping a heavy sack of clothes down the street in the snow, or realizing a pair of dirty underwear was shoved right up against the viewable edge of the partially sheer sack fabric as you waited with a throng of people at an intersection, or schlepping it all the way down only to realize that you've forgotten your laundry charge card, or at least the $10 bill required to recharge it, I suppose it wasn't so bad.

Post Office

The plus side to having a post office literally around the corner from your apartment seems pretty obvious. Such convenience. And even though the busyness of the city and the resulting increase of people in the lines cancels out the benefit of the large number of windows open in a Manhattan post office, you still somehow feel like things move faster. The downside, however, to having a post office literally around the corner is that when mailing a package, you have to schlep it down multiple flights of stairs, down the street, and around said corner instead of simply out your front door and into the car that's sitting in your driveway. It's true, the post office may be close in Manhattan, but you'll have to carry anything you want to mail every step of the way.

Dry Cleaner

My dry cleaning establishment was steps from my apartment building, a dirty little shop filled from floor to ceiling with pressed and folded clothes wrapped in tightly bound paper packaging. I loved looking at all those packages, thinking it must be satisfying to fetch the correct package when a customer brought in his ticket. These tickets were the basis of all transactions, with rarely a word spoken between me and the Asian dry cleaner as I handed over my ticket and he came back a moment later with my clothes. If it weren't so expensive, I'd have had him clean *everything* I ever wore.

Bakery

The neighborhood bakery was, oddly, one I could never quite get on board with. Mostly because the sweets never drew me in. They just never looked very, well, *sweet*. Give me cakes, give me pies. Give me fancy-cut confections laced with powdered sugar and frosting. Or at least something that looks like it's more than just a different way of making bread. And that's the impression I got every time I stepped inside. I'd vow that this time I would purchase something, and yet I almost always left empty handed, dreaming about the baked goods from the shop several blocks away. I confess I cheated on my neighborhood bakery with this shop many, many times. For this I am sorry. For not being sorry.

The best way I can describe it then is that a Manhattan neighborhood is the group of people all using the same locations of these business types as their own; the group of people who used the same grocery store, laundromat, post office, dry cleaner, and bakery as I did. Maybe down the street from the grocery store there was another grocery store, or another dry cleaner half a block away from the one I went to. But those were for other groups of people; groups that together formed other neighborhoods with those who frequented other sets of grocery stores, laundromats, post offices, dry cleaners, and bakeries.

I'm not sure why this whole neighborhood concept was so important for me to identify. It's not as if I pictured my neighbors and I collaborating on bake sales and carpools. It's not even that I wondered about my options when I needed to borrow a cup of sugar. It wasn't as romantic as that. But I did find myself thinking about these neighbors often, wondering who they were and how much space it would take up if everyone in the neighborhood came out front and joined hands for a moment, all of us smiling together over the new washing machines at the laundromat and shaking our heads at the overabundance of regular bread at the bakery. Because who *were* the people with whom I could have these kinds of conversations?

The answer, I suppose, is that they were the ones waiting with me in the laundromat. The ones whose clothes filled the paper packages on the dry cleaner's wall. The ones making the grocery store aisles seem extra narrow. The ones not demanding nearly enough sweets from the baker. We shared this piece of New York in just this way, see. And isn't that something? Staring from my window at the apartment buildings on the other side of the street, didn't we have this thing, whatever it was, together, here, that could never be replicated? I'd like to think we did. And not just because they had probably all at some point seen my underwear smashed against the side of my laundry sack while waiting behind me at an intersection.

GOING

AT FIRST, HARLEM INTIMIDATED ME. THIS IS mostly because it felt a little unsafe and I wasn't used to being the only white person on a given block or neighborhood.

In truth, I didn't have much experience with black people. Raised in a small western town where there were almost quite literally none, I moved on to small college towns that were just as shockingly white.

My first experience being a minority myself, from a sheer population standpoint, was when I finished graduate school and took a job in Cleveland. It's probably still considered the Midwest, technically, but Cleveland to me felt incredibly east. I was *so far east*. In the Eastern Standard Time zone, for crying out loud. And a flight to Manhattan only took an hour.

I arrived in Cleveland on a plane with my mother, who'd come to help me settle in. Waiting for my car and belongings to arrive via the moving company my new employer had sprung for, we busied ourselves using my relocation money* to purchase the things I'd need in my new house. I can still remember stopping in my tracks in the middle of the Cleveland Heights Walmart as it dawned on me that my mother and I were the only two white people in the entire store. And Walmart is not a small store.

"Are we supposed to *be here?*" I finally asked my mom quietly, both of us standing there swiveling our heads.

I'm not sure what I was getting at, because surely there wasn't an entirely separate Walmart for us white folk, and certainly I knew that. Yet so startled was I by the complete lack of anyone else who looked like us that I felt compelled to at least ask the question.

There *were* white people in Cleveland, a fact I discovered when I showed up at my new job in a nice office building in the suburbs. My office was, in fact, almost exclusively white, a fact that's always bothered me, given that every single worker at every single restaurant, grocery store, and gas station near my home was black. Any social structure that's this rigged, that makes it much more possible for white people to have the good-paying, benefit-riddled jobs seems pretty messed up.

These thoughts bubbled to the forefront again after I settled in Harlem, a place I'd moved to flee the much higher

---

*My number one tip for anyone looking to increase her earning potential, or even simply the number of job-related perks she enjoys, i.e. free money, is to get an MBA.

rent prices in the mostly white Upper East Side. So I was saving almost $1,000 per month, and all my neighbors were black. Again, I'm uncomfortable with a structure that makes it more possible for white people to be able to afford higher rents, which may be why I quickly became more comfortable living in Harlem than I had ever been on the Upper East Side. I no longer felt privileged, I just felt like a regular person. To be honest, I felt a little *less* than regular—I was unemployed, on an Obamacare health plan, and ate a lot of ramen noodles and canned ravioli—but I found Harlem to be much more accepting, in that it allowed me to become a part of everything, to feel more like I was living, to embrace what was going on around me.

True that I had to walk further to get where I wanted to go in Harlem. Not the subway, which was thankfully much closer, but everything else. The grocery store was nine blocks away instead of one. The post office was no longer around the corner. Getting to the gym took ten minutes instead of two.

Doing laundry was especially different. Not only because I had to lug my dirty clothes much further, but also because the increased distance to and from my apartment meant it no longer made sense to go back while I waited for the clothes to wash and dry. Admittedly, there was a part of me that felt there was also a greater chance of someone absconding with my clothes if I wasn't there to keep watch. Either way, I spent much more time at the laundromat while living in Harlem.

Unlike the sterile, almost factory-like rows of silver machines at my old laundromat, the one closest to me in Harlem felt like a vacation. Or like it was trying to be. The owner was always there, a foreign woman taking payments at the front counter for things like detergent and dry-cleaned clothes. The place was colorful, had an island vibe, and radio music played from a low-budget sound system. Despite the uncomfortable blue metal chairs, it's the kind of place that made you want to stay, and how odd is that for a laundromat? I'd try and read a book but end up distracted by the music and spend most of my wash and dry cycles thinking about that fact that I lived here. In Manhattan. In Harlem. How strange it all was that this is how they did things here. That this was my life. It both delighted and surprised me.

There is a mural painted on a wall near 125th Street that I'd often pass while walking home to my apartment on 119th. "Spirit of Harlem," I learned when I looked it up. The mural captures a jazz scene, musicians and singers and dancers, all dressed up, all just feeling and enjoying the beat. I caught myself staring at it a lot, wanting to grab on to one of the colorful blocks of blue or yellow and transport myself to a place that was so carefree, so lively, so beautiful. Then the signal would change and I'd join the throngs of others crossing the same street, our steps on the pavement creating another kind of beat, one equally as beautiful.

SIDEBAR: CELEBRITIES AND
HOW TO SEE THEM

When it comes down to it, you can divide life into two segments. There is life before you have seen George Clooney in person, and there is life after you have seen George Clooney in person. There's really no other way to slice it. But I'm getting ahead of myself.

In my early experiences with New York City, I had celebrities all wrong. I wanted to see them, these people I saw looking so glamorous on TV and in magazines, and so I scoured the city streets looking for them. I wanted to see them doing regular, real-life things. Like picking up baguettes and cheese at the corner market, enjoying brunch with groups of friends, walking their dogs in the park, leaving the gym after a workout. I knew they did these things, and

so I adopted a permanent filter where I processed all faces I came across looking for any that seemed familiar.

It took me a while to realize that my filter was set to 'Fancy.' Because it's how I pictured them in my mind, I had been scouring the streets looking for the best-dressed people I could find; those dripping with labels, large sunglasses on regardless of weather, and an overall aura of sparkle that could be attributed to nothing in particular.

Of course, the trouble with this filter is that most celebrities don't want to be recognized while they do regular, real-life things. Most celebrities look quite normal when out and about. Which is why I didn't at first realize that the ponytailed woman perusing the same table of shoes at Lord & Taylor one day was none other than Alexis Bledel. Wearing yoga pants and a sweatshirt, my Fancy filter would have never picked her up. She wasn't even wearing makeup. But it was obviously her, and I was transfixed.

I hung around the shoe department for over an hour, watching her shop. I couldn't figure out why no one else in the store seemed to realize what was going on. Not even the salesperson helping her. None of them were saying hello, telling her how much they loved *Gilmore Girls*, or asking for a picture. To this day I'm really not sure if it's because no one realized it was her or no one cared (maybe this sort of thing happens all the time when you live in New York?), but I certainly didn't want to be the *only* one making a fuss or blowing her cover. And so I ogled from a distance until she left.

This type of celebrity run-in is what I call a Type 1. It's the best of all run-ins, in that it's not planned or ticketed.

It's you seeing a celebrity out in the world doing something not at all related to being a celebrity. It's completely random and unexpected. It's delightful. It's Katie Holmes walking down the street right toward you. It's Dolly Parton at the airport. And yes, it's shoe shopping with Alexis Bledel.

There are two other types of run-ins that can be equally satisfying but are far less charming. A Type 2 celebrity sighting still involves seeing a celebrity when you hadn't known you would, but it's due to you putting yourself in a situation or vicinity where the odds of seeing a celebrity are higher. Running into Jim Gaffigan as he filmed a segment for his show was a Type 2 run-in. I hadn't planned it, but he was being a celebrity and was surrounded by a crowd of people. Watching from the front of the line at a Broadway show when Angela Lansbury was escorted into the theater was a Type 2 run-in as well. I didn't know I would see her, but I was at a Broadway show, so the chances of seeing someone notable were increased.

And then there are Type 3 run-ins—those that are full-on planned. The deck is stacked in this case, in that you have *planned* to be where you *know* a certain celebrity is. Seeing Ryan Seacrest in Times Square on New Year's Eve was a Type 3 run-in. So was seeing Daniel Radcliffe perform in *How to Succeed in Business Without Really Trying*. Its Type 3-ness didn't diminish my glee (Harry Potter sings!), but I'd bought a ticket. I could spend an entire chapter chronicling all the celebrities I've seen this way. No doubt we all could.

Indeed, most of the run-ins we have are Type 3, in the form of concerts and shows where we buy a ticket and are guaranteed an evening in the presence of a certain celebrity.

And in the case of George Clooney, while it would be cooler if the whole thing had happened organically, his was a Type 3 run-in as well.

People outside of big cities might not know this, but there are websites devoted solely to the posting of movie shoot locations. So if you've got a day to kill in Manhattan and want to see who you can see, just hop onto one of these sites and see if any of the flicks being filmed on that day strike your fancy. Which is exactly what a couple girlfriends and I did on the afternoon we saw George Clooney.

He was filming *Money Monster* over on Wall Street, and it really wasn't very hard at all to secure ourselves a spot along a nearby sidewalk. We were among many others, all standing on tip toes and shuffling angles to maximize our line of sight to George, who was a ways down the road filming the scene where he is walking down the street while wearing the supposed vest of dynamite.

I was so wrapped up in trying to catch a glimpse of what was happening down the street that I didn't realize a black SUV had pulled up to the curb right next to me. I was so wrapped up in tracking where George was that I didn't realize he was walking right toward me. I then became so wrapped up in getting a close-up picture of him that I completely lost my cool and got what can only be described as a terribly blurry picture of George Clooney.

What struck me, aside from how mad at myself I was for botching what would have been such a great picture—him literally right in front of me, jacket off, his sexy graying hair the same shade as the vest of his three-piece suit—was how attractive he is.

Groundbreaking, I know.

But I'm telling you. It's different when you're *there*. When you're *seeing* him. It reminded me of the first time I saw the Counting Crows in concert. The favorite band of most of my immediate family members, the first time we saw them live, a sibling leaned over to me during the opening number and said of lead singer Adam Duritz, "I didn't know he could *sing*."

Having spent years listening to their albums, it seemed a ridiculous thing to say. Of course he could sing. And of course we knew he could sing. Yet I understood. I understood exactly. It was *different* somehow. It was better. It was exquisite. And it was something we never would have known relying on recorded albums alone.

And so it was with George Clooney that day on Wall Street. Him being attractive is simply fact, I knew it already. But seeing him in person was disarming. Affecting. The man is disarmingly, affectingly attractive. And if you'll promise not to lose all respect for me, I'm not sure I've been the same since.

Jodie Foster, the film's director, was busy running between a few different vantage points as they filmed, but it hardly seemed worth the effort to photograph her.* I wanted George back. By this time he'd of course gotten into the black SUV and been driven away, and I was left part sulking, part wistful over the now George-less cast that remained to finish the scene.

It's my favorite celebrity run-in to date, and I've got the picture to prove it. You can't tell it's George, but I know. I know the truth about this second segment of life. And someday when it happens to you, you'll know, too.

---

*Even though I did anyway and got a really great shot.

COMING

THE TROUBLE STARTED A COUPLE OF WEEKS after arriving in New York.

I'd spent a few days out west on a recruiting trip for my company, the first time I'd left the city since becoming one of its residents. I remember rolling the window down on the late-night taxi ride home from the airport. It was fall, crisp, and the skyline was a beautiful blur of lights in between bridges.

Satisfying, that's what it was. To be coming home to New York.

To be dropped off in front of my own building. To check the mail in the lobby, walk up the stairs of the always-lit hallway, and turn the key in the door that opened to my own little corner of the city.

For so long I had wanted this. I had hoped it would feel just this way, and it did. It felt like living.

With my suitcase open in the middle of the floor and my cat bouncing around in her exuberance at having me home, I began unpacking. Within a few minutes there was a sharp pounding sound coming from below me. It was startling in the way something is when you feel your heart beating in your throat, and violating in the way something is when you feel called out for something you have every right to be doing.

Because what exactly *was* I doing? I was *unpacking my suitcase*. Hardly an act that seemed worthy of such reprimand. Yet my neighbor had just broomed her ceiling at me. For several moments I sat frozen on the floor, kneeling in front of the suitcase. Had I been unpacking loudly? Too much walking back and forth between closet and suitcase and dresser? Was 11:00 at night too late to be subjecting my downstairs neighbor to this many footsteps, even if they were soft ones made by a very skinny girl who was wearing slippers?

I went to bed right away, the brooming having killed the New Yorky high I'd been riding since landing a couple of hours earlier. It took me a few days to realize that the brooming, which from then on became a very regular thing, happened only when my cat was running around.

Did you hear what I said?

My *cat*.

Who weighed all of five pounds.

And slept twenty hours a day.

Yet it soon became clear that my neighbor had a vendetta against me and my cat and was hell bent on making sure I knew about it. She'd *rap rap rap* with the broom handle, she'd yell up at me through her ceiling, she'd shout obscenities through the stairwell. Nevermind that my cat was only active for a few brief periods each day. Or that the rest of the day and night I was surely the quietest neighbor this woman would ever have. Nevermind that comparing the sounds of a five-pound tabby to the gallop of a "jungle tiger cat" is not even remotely acceptable or accurate.

True, the walls were thin. Like many apartment buildings in New York City, mine was an old one, with paper-like walls that didn't do much to keep you from knowing exactly what your neighbors were up to. The lady in the apartment next to mine, for instance, worked mostly from home, and all day long I heard her thick Brooklyn accent on various conference calls, as well as the TV shows she watched in between.

And on the other side of my bathroom was my landlord's bathroom, the apartment where she and her husband lived being a complete mirror image of mine. You'll have to trust me on this, but if there's one room where you'd really prefer to *not* hear the sounds others make, it's the bathroom. Even worse than bedroom noises, bathroom noises are a particularly uncomfortable combination of intimate and gross. And if you think hearing, in perfect clarity, your landlord's husband draw a bath, remove his clothes, step into the water, and utter a contented sigh once submerged doesn't affect your ability to complete your business while on the toilet, then you're kidding yourself.

This is all to say that I don't doubt that the woman who lived below me could hear my cat. The same way I could hear when there was movement in the apartment above me. But when you live in New York City, it's simply part of the drill. And the woman below me, who I learned had lived in that apartment for something like thirty years, surely understood this. Surely she understood that on the spectrum of noisy neighbors, I was on the least offending end.

I could have listened to loud music, been part of a band that rehearsed in my apartment, had a live-in boyfriend whom I loudly loved, worn stilettos, had a crying baby, had a barking dog, or any number of things that made me exponentially louder than I actually was. And as the battle between us raged (basically her yelling and brooming and me feeling increasingly stressed and defeated), many of my New York friends suggested I become much noisier, revenge-style, in an effort to really piss her off.

One afternoon when I became particularly enraged after enduring a bout of her brooming and yelling, I decided to dip my toe in the water. I began stomping and jumping around the apartment, each step ripe with anger and bitterness as it hit the floor with as much force as I could muster. I felt possessed. The way you feel when you know you should stop, when you know you aren't being you, when you know you'll regret it, but my feet hitting the floor felt addicting in the way something is when it feels too good to stop.

It probably only lasted a minute or so, this outburst, and you can bet the lady downstairs reacted instantly.

"Hey!" she shouted up at me.

"Heeeeyyyyyy!" I heard louder as I kept stomping.

And then, with the desperation of a banshee.

"WHAAAAAAAT IIIIIIS THAAAAAAAT? HEEEEEEEEEEEEYYYYYYYYYYYYYYY!"

Your move, bitch.

GOING

NEW YORK IS AN OLD CITY. SO THERE'S NOT
much you'll glean from the somewhat less than earth-shat-
tering statement that many of the apartment buildings
everyone's living in are also old. Certainly much older than
the sprawling suburbia cookie-cutters the rest of America
calls home.

I never asked either of my landlords exactly how old the
buildings were. My Upper East Side studio was like many
of the other buildings it was sandwiched next to—narrow,
modest in height (only four stories), and updated only in
those ways that keep it fully functional. It was what I'd call a
typical apartment building, laid out in a typical apartments/
stairwell/apartments/stairwell pattern, such that every floor
looked identical. Sometimes I actually lost track of what

floor I was on and had to stop and look at the numbers on the doors.

My Harlem apartment on the other hand was like something out of a movie. Something with character oozing out of the dark banisters. A building equal parts beautiful and creepy, it was clear there had been far less done to it over the decades by way of upkeep, but it consequently seemed more authentic. Here was some *real* New York; an example of the detail and creativity with which buildings used to be constructed. Here was *history*.

When I'd first looked at the building, the landlord showed me the rather stunning apartment belonging to the man on the first floor. I was considering renting the apartment above his, so who this person was (after the horrid experience with the cat-hating woman below me) was a matter of no small importance. The occupant, a tall and very thin man in his fifties whom I never saw without a fedora on his head, seemed perfectly pleasant, but what relieved me even more than his carefree demeanor was just how high his ceiling was. It was positively cavernous. It would be physically impossible then for him to broom the ceiling at me.

As I smiled up at what would mean a broom-free existence, I began to notice the actual ceiling itself, which was a beautiful ivory color and carved into a spectacular pattern of texture and shape. The kind of ceiling you'd see in a museum or a concert hall, and here someone had gone to such care and effort for a mere apartment building. Or perhaps a hotel, if that's what it had been in a previous life. The thin, fedora-wearing man had lived there for a small eternity, and even so had only decorated sparsely. He slept on a mattress that sat in one corner of the floor. What an odd existence, and in a rather fascinating building.

It wasn't just the architecture that was strange in the Harlem building—the ornate ceilings, the wide staircases, the lack of lighting in the halls and entryway—it was how the landlord ran the place. Our mail, for instance, wasn't divvied up into individual locked boxes that we each opened at our leisure. Rather, the daily mail for the entire building was placed in a heap on a small shelf in the entryway. Such that we had to shuffle through the whole stack searching for those items addressed to us each time we passed. It was part charming, maybe, in some sort of communal way, but mostly it induced a healthy amount of paranoia. Not that I had any reason to distrust any of my neighbors in particular, but still, the odds of getting important pieces of mail do decrease when there are many hands rifling through it. And it always seemed incredibly likely to me that a neighbor would take something addressed to me—whether on purpose or by accident.

And when rent came due each month, the landlord, who lived in the building next door, asked us to place our checks in a little wire basket adhered to the gate outside. *Outside.* He wanted us to leave our checks *outside.* In a *basket.* In the *open.* That *anyone* could reach into. Between the mail and the rent checks, it all just seemed so trusting. And as a single girl living alone in Harlem, if there's one thing I wasn't, it was trusting.

Within the first few days of moving into the Harlem building, I did get curious about what the rest of the building was like. Between the cavernous first-floor apartment and the dark, foreboding hallways, I wanted to see what else might be in store for the tenants, so I tiptoed up an extra floor. That's really all there was, just three floors, maybe nine apartments, and other than a general sense of creepiness (mostly from the lack of lighting), the only thing that had me stumped was a partially open door about halfway down the third-floor hallway.

It didn't seem likely that someone had left their apartment door open, so it couldn't be that. A closet, maybe? Something maintenance related? I pushed the door cautiously and saw that the small room contained a toilet and a shower, neither very inviting. So this was a *bathroom*? A random bathroom on the third floor? I suddenly worried that maybe some tenant had reign of the entire third floor and that I'd be caught snooping around their bathroom.

Hurrying downstairs to the safety of my own apartment, I didn't give much additional thought to the random third-floor bathroom until a few weeks later when I ran into my neighbor walking into his apartment wearing nothing but a towel around his waist. Clearly just out of the shower, it suddenly dawned on me that not all the apartments in the building had a bathroom. Could this really be true? Was this still a thing in modern adult society? This dormitory, hostel-like life that saw a person leaving the confines of his own apartment every time he so much as needed to pee?

Even for less rent, I wasn't sure how that was an acceptable tradeoff, a stance I held firmly as I got down from my loft bed night after night to pad the few steps over to my very own bathroom. Some things a girl just needs.

Coming

EVEN AT THE TIME WHEN MY DIRECTOR BOSS
agreed to let me move to New York and work remotely,
he'd hinted that it wasn't a good long-term solution. And
by hinted, I mean that he told me. In those exact words. So
I'd always known this was an arrangement that would end,
likely sooner rather than later.

Not that this really bothered me. All I was concerned
about was getting to New York and being employed as I got
settled and prepared for my next career move, which, if you
know me at all, shouldn't come as any surprise. I had jewelry
on the brain, see. I always had. And my master plan with
relocating was to become a gemologist, as my gemology
school had a campus in Manhattan.

Even with these new life plans in the works, I enjoyed my
time working remotely from New York for Pressure-Sensitive

Leader immensely, and the thought of this time expiring made me a little bit sad. Not just because of the flexibility that working from home provides, both in terms of working hours* and location.** But also because of the girl about town reception I got whenever I was in Cleveland for business at headquarters.

By this time I'd gotten a pixie cut, and the reaction back in the Midwest was quite mixed. Not that anyone, other than a certain family member, ever told me to my face that I should never cut my hair like that again. But when people react with comments about how brave you are and how different it is from your previous hairstyle rather than about your hair actually looking good, it's safe to assume they think you've made a horrible mistake.

But there were some who raved. One of the most beautiful and stylish women in the whole office made a point of sending me an email about how great I looked in a pixie. Not that I didn't look good before, she was quick to clarify, but now I was "stunning." You hear that? *Stunning.* The *Pretty Woman* word. How many times has someone used it to describe how a haircut has changed *your* look? Or how *anything* has changed your look?

And so I walked a little taller down the halls of our Cleveland office, knowing whether or not people liked my haircut that I was still pretty badass for having done it. I was still the one they were letting work remotely from New York City. I was still the one whose entrance into a conference

---

*Out late? Sleep in until noon and work until 8.

**Feel like a change of scene? Schlep your laptop to your favorite Starbucks or diner of choice while you crunch numbers over fried eggs and toast.

room meeting prompted the Marketing Communications manager to play "Uptown Girl" over the speakers.

Of course, I was also the one they were preparing to replace. On one visit I found they'd already hired the girl. I hadn't seen a single resume or participated in a single interview. No one had sought my advice on the choice of successor, or even bothered to tell me at all. Not that a company has any such obligation to an employee who is on her way out, but it still felt like a slight. A feeling that was hard to shake as I returned to New York and began to train the girl, a fresh MBA grad—I had also been a fresh MBA grad when I'd started at the company almost seven years before—over a series of phone conversations.

The day of my goodbye happy hour—chosen on what was likely to be my last trip to Cleveland while employed by Pressure-Sensitive Leader—ended up being a complete weather shit show. A horrid snowstorm made it almost impossible for me to get my piddly rental car to the bar, and most people who had planned to come ended up bailing on account of the poor road conditions. I'd like to say I understood, or that it didn't bother me, but I just get so damn sentimental about things that mean something to me; people who mean something to me. And I wanted everyone to show up for me the way I had shown up for everyone in the past, wishing various people well as they left for better jobs, decided to stay home with their babies, or fell in love and moved across the country.

I had to settle for the few, the brave, the faithful co-workers who endured the snow that night to have a beer in my honor, and maybe that was enough. Maybe it could fill the strange and unsettling void I was fighting inside, knowing as I flew back to New York that I would never see most of the people in that office building ever again. Should it have mattered? All the customer service reps and finance workers and business development gurus I waited in line with in the cafeteria, sat next to in training meetings, exchanged a few words with at the company clam bake. Was I losing something? Were they?

I stayed on for a few more months from New York, training my replacement while continuing to run my little product line. My last day was chosen purposefully—it was the one I had to work until in order to receive my full bonus for the previous year.* I sent some final emails and then gathered all the things that belonged to the office—a laptop, a phone, and a company credit card—and headed to the post office.

It was a short walk, the closest post office to my apartment being just around the corner, so I moved my feet slowly, pausing for a moment to call my Director Boss from the phone I was about to mail back to him and say goodbye. I'd loved working for him so much, but it wasn't just that. It's that the entire seven years had for the most part been such a good experience. And here I was, choosing to leave. Here I was, already gone. I'd like to think he couldn't hear the emotion in my voice as I kept it brief, casual, unsentimental. I'd like to think he didn't notice when I abruptly ended the call due to the way my throat stuck when I said the final, "Goodbye."

I was standing under a tree, stalling, watching the cars

---

*I'm no fool.

and taxis speed by as I cried for the job and boss I no longer had. What must he have thought from this final conversation—me, standing on a noisy street outside of a post office barely holding it together. Did he feel bad for me? Jobless and clearly emotional about it. He didn't know about my gemology plan, of course, but he must have worried about me, this man who for Christmas had mailed me a huge box of granola bars and squeezy applesauce pouches, either because he knew I liked them or because he thought of me as about to be poor and starving. It's a toss-up.

Opening the door to the post office, I dropped the phone into the box I'd already halfway packed and sealed it up, pausing only for a moment to close my eyes and take a breath. Then I stepped into the line to wait for the clerk to call for the next customer, suddenly wondering what kind of adhesive the USPS used on their shipping labels.

GOING

THE MAIN DIFFERENCE BETWEEN MY OLD APART~
ment on the Upper East Side and my new one in Harlem—
besides the drastic change in location, surroundings, and
people—was that my old apartment had been furnished.
Remember my epic Cleveland garage sale? I had gotten rid
of 90 percent of what I owned, not only because I would no
longer have room for it, but also because I would no longer
need it. My Upper East Side apartment came stocked with
everything from a bed, couch, dresser, TV, and desk, to
dishes, towels, bedding, utensils, and cleaning supplies.

Which meant that my new apartment in Harlem was
glaringly empty.

Aside from the loft bed, a rather Herculean wooden
thing complete with protective slats surrounding the divot

meant for a mattress, the only thing in the entire apartment was a large white desk that the previous occupants had left behind. They asked if I was interested, and knowing it could function as a writing desk, gemology workstation, and kitchen table, I quickly said yes. Or maybe it's that I suddenly found myself cast in the role of Girl Who Owns Nothing, and Girl Who Owns Nothing But A Desk seemed like a small but important step up.

The living area in my new apartment had shiny hardwood floors and a high ceiling. The window in the front let in a good deal of sun, and if you were facing it, the loft bed was against the right wall and the white desk was against the left. The apartment had no closets, so I turned the space created by the high loft bed into one. A rod had been fashioned and fixed at the top of the space, creating a perfect place for hanging things. And while the couple who'd lived there before had me completely enchanted by the way they'd disguised the makeshift closet behind a beaded pastel curtain, I had no such creative ability. Everyone who came into my Harlem apartment could see everything I had in my open-door closet.

Whereas my old apartment had contained everything—living area, sleeping area, kitchen, and bathroom—all within the same rectangle of space, the new apartment was actually a bit sectioned off. The living and sleeping areas were together, but behind them the hardwood ended, and through a small doorway was a tiled kitchen area. An *actual* kitchen, which felt like a luxury. Even though there were no dishes, utensils, pots, or pans. Not even a microwave. And I'd still be battling a pesky gas oven and washing dishes by hand. But still, a real kitchen.

At the back of the kitchen on the right, there was a door down a short hallway that led to a long and narrow bathroom. It looked like it had been rather awkwardly configured based on the strange amount of space the contractors saw they had left to work with. A toilet sat at the far end, a shower at the near end, with a long space connecting them. And the bathroom was painted a very dark maroon with a strip of maroon and white floral wallpaper down the center. There were even inspiring quotes from foreign philosophers written in lacy handwriting scattered over the wall's surface. Not exactly the area of a home that I'd most want to turn into a beautiful, inspiring niche, but the landlord told me the couple who'd moved out had been particularly involved in and proud of the bathroom design. Whatever does it for you, I guess.

I'd been sleeping on my air mattress since moving in, as I no longer owned a bed. The wooden loft frame did simplify things, in that all I really had to get was a mattress. Which I did rather fortuitously when a friend down the street received two in the mail from IKEA as opposed to the one he had ordered. I paid him the retail price of the brand new mattress, and even though a part of me felt like payment wasn't necessary since he had paid all of *nothing* for this duplicate mattress, he did deliver it right to me, schlepping it over his shoulder for the nine blocks between our apartments.

So now I had a mattress and a desk.

Realizing I needed to buy a whole lot more, and cheaply, I did what any girl on a budget in a new apartment would do. I went to Target.

The Target nearest me was a mile and a half away, which I walked, and then preceded to fill a cart with those things I felt were the bare minimum needed to get by in my little apartment: one towel, one washcloth, one dish towel, one pot, one pan, one spatula, one plastic stirring spoon, one mixing bowl, two plastic tumblers, one baking sheet, a shower curtain, a broom, a dustpan, a folding chair for my desk/lab/table, and probably a few other things I'm forgetting.

It felt like a lot, my full cart, and I began to dread how much it all would cost. Looking rather forlornly at all the items as I waited in line, items I'd owned a mere year before, I thought back to a conversation I'd had with a family member around the time of my garage sale in Cleveland. Discussing everything I was parting with, she paused at one point and finally asked what I think she'd wanted to all along.

"But aren't you going to *need* silverware? And measuring cups, and mixing bowls? Aren't you going to want to have all these things you're getting rid of?"

It was a fair point that I think referred less to my immediate move—the furnished, fully-stocked apartment that awaited me in New York—and more to the fact that I wasn't going to live there forever. And what would I do then? I'd thought about this too back when I was getting rid of everything, but the hard truth was that I simply couldn't take it with me. And I refused to put everything I owned in a storage unit for the duration of my time in Manhattan.

Miraculously, my total at Target that day only came to $85. Just think about that for a second. Going from zero to functional in a new apartment for only $85. I felt almost giddy as I began walking home, excited to put each new thing in its proper place, a giddiness that began to taper only as I realized that walking a mile and a half with your arms loaded down with new apartment things is difficult, especially when one of them is a broom and one of them is a freaking folding chair. I began stopping every two minutes to rearrange and ultimately settled on the broom balancing over my shoulder and the folding chair upside down and hooked onto the broomstick, both my arms battling multiple bags.

It's something people living anywhere else take for granted—the ability to transport things they acquire on any given shopping trip. But let me assure you that when you can only transport what you can carry on your own person, it really changes the game. It's the reason I'd resorted to buying seven-pound bags of cat litter at the supermarket instead of forty-two-pound bags at Costco. It's the reason I got groceries in smaller, more frequent trips. And it's the reason I looked like a total freak that day walking home from Target hauling a chair hanging off of a broom handle.

Not that anyone so much as batted an eye. Just another Saturday on the island.

SIDEBAR: SWEET TREATS AND HOW TO GET WRITTEN INTO MY WILL

On my first night living in Manhattan, I had walked over to Carnegie Deli for some cheesecake. Some *New York* cheesecake, which is what you spend your life ordering in all cities *other* than New York so you can feel a part of it all from wherever you are.

Carnegie Deli wasn't exactly right next door. It was a more than two mile walk, each way, but it was a cool fall evening, I'd just moved in, and I wanted to do something New Yorky. That, and the subway intimidated me. Only for a little while, mind you, but on this first night as New Yorker, I was the epitome of green. Or make that, *shit, did I just move to New York City?*

New York cheesecake is plain, bare, and usually comes with that ever-so-slight sour cream layer at the top. Strawberry or cherry topping is usually available as an optional add-on. For wimps. A lifelong fan of cheesecake, particularly of the plain, bare, topping-less variety, I was struck that evening that it turns out I like New York cheesecake less than almost any other kind of cheesecake, even the recipe we got from our high school German teacher that our family has been using ever since. Truly one of the best things to come out of the public education system in southern Oregon.

Say what you will about Carnegie Deli's cheesecake (I prefer Junior's, or, better yet, Two Little Red Hens), but one positively delectable takeaway from my time in New York is the plethora of treats that are available to you. And no one is as shocked as I am that I didn't gain a crap ton of weight while living in the city. I have the East Side to thank for the fact that it was a mile round trip just to the subway and back. I felt like I was constantly burning calories that could then be re-consumed in the form of something sweet.

I was a sucker for the popular places, but that's because they're *good*. No matter how many celebrities mention Levain Bakery, or how many tourists post selfies of themselves there because Taylor Swift tweeted about it, that doesn't change the fact that *the cookies at Levain Bakery are amazing*. Not that I can say I've tried even the tiniest fraction of all the cookies in all the boroughs, but once I found Levain, I sort of stopped looking.

Their model is simple, and they only sell four kinds of cookie. Chocolate chip walnut, dark chocolate chocolate chip, and dark chocolate peanut butter chip make up the first three. Not a huge chocolate fan myself, I'm loyal to the fourth and final cookie, the oatmeal raisin. Not a particular favorite of mine in any other circumstance—who hasn't come across a potluck cookie platter with everything gone except for the oatmeal raisin?—the oatmeal raisin at Levain is something special.

For starters, it doesn't have that offending and often times overwhelming cinnamon thing going on. It's just plain dough with oats and raisins. And of all the four cookie varieties at Levain, the oatmeal raisin is the thickest. It stands up the tallest, bakes the highest, and contains the most gooey goodness inside. Even if you don't generally care for oatmeal raisin, try this cookie. And then get back to me. Levain's main location is on the Upper West Side, near where my church congregation met. And while a hallmark of people of my faith—devout, super strict people of my faith—is that the Sabbath should be devoid of activities you could easily do on another day, like shopping or eating out, it was hard to resist stopping on the way home from church each week. I'd swing that paper bag along Central Park West and ultimately indulge while sitting on the crosstown bus ride home. I mean, if God didn't want me to shop on Sunday, he surely wouldn't have put my church so close to Levain Bakery.

The other bakery I visited with alarming regularity was Dominique Ansel's little gem on Spring Street. He's widely attributed with inventing the cronut, a craze if ever there was one, and even now, if you go to his website, you'll find you still have to reserve one well in advance. And what better way to both keep your product in demand and make your bakery a must-visit tourist stop than developing a delicious new pastry that is half croissant, half donut and only making a limited number of them per day?

For those not lucky enough to secure a reserved cronut, there's a line that forms where you can wait for one of the surplus cronuts made that day. At some point in the morning, sometimes still very early, they run out, but of all the times I stood in line hoping to get one, I can't remember ever being turned away. It means dragging your sweet and sour out the door at 7:00 in the morning, and it also means feeling like complete crap afterward for having overloaded yourself with sheer sweetness, but it's worth it to participate in this thing you know not everyone is getting. Worth it to see what the never-repeating flavor that month will be. And to open that yellow box and know you're not going to stop until you've licked the last of the sugar from your fingers.

Magnolia Bakery is the one I could never quite get on board with, mostly because a red velvet cupcake—one of my favorites and a downright bakery staple—should be unequivocally delicious. Theirs simply was not. Frankly, I went to Sprinkles most often for red velvet, and they aren't even unique to New York. Magnolia's banana pudding is worth trying, but most of the time when I went to one of their locations, I left completely underwhelmed.

I can't say the same of Serendipity, a favorite—if not a silly one—of mine. It's part that John Cusack movie, of course, a little that scene in *One Fine Day* when Michelle Pfeiffer and the kids are passing huge ice cream dishes back and forth across the table, but mostly it's the naughty knick-knacks for sale in the lobby. I'm kidding, of course. It's *all* the naughty knickknacks for sale in the lobby. No, it's not. I'm still kidding.

The fact is, frozen hot chocolate is just a good idea. Frozen white hot chocolate might be an even better idea. And that Serendipity is really the only place that's selling it means one has to go there. And so I went. A lot. They have food, too—and did I mention the knickknacks?—but that's not really why you go. You go for something sweet and frozen. Period.

The Serendipity menu, which is large and cluttered and a complete delight to look through, contains something called the $1,000 Sundae.* I think the literal gold shavings that top the ice cream is what does the trick, but if you give them three days' notice, you and a guest can enjoy the $1,000 Sundae together, hopefully at a more glamorous table than the one right by the restroom.

My friend Molly and I had a plan to go and order that sundae if either one of us ever hit it big. If some super significant life event made us feel like we had achieved either notoriety or at least a large influx of cash that we didn't feel irresponsible about spending on ice cream. Neither of us have ever felt like we've gotten to that point, but it's still the plan. We talked about the $1,000 Sundae so much while living in New York that even though we've both now moved back west, I went ahead and wrote her into my will—enough cash so she can fly herself to New York from wherever she's living and enjoy the sundae in my honor. I wouldn't go so far as to say I almost hope I die so she can have the sundae (too much?), but in the event of my early demise, it's a small yet significant silver lining to me. I can picture her seated at an upstairs table holding a spoonful of vanilla and gold shavings skyward before digging in.

I hope it's delicious.

---

*Since I moved away, it's been renamed The Golden Opulence Sundae which, I'm sorry, is a way worse name.

COMING

IN ORDER TO BECOME A GEMOLOGIST, YOU'LL need to own several pieces of equipment. These are, for the most part, small items, but necessary nonetheless. The goal of becoming a gemologist, after all, is to get to a point where you can identify any gemstone. Rough, faceted, cabochon. No matter what it is, someone could bring it to you and your arsenal of tools would, like a little investigation, ultimately yield a correct identification. In fact, the final test before receiving a graduate gemology diploma involves being assigned a random box of gemstones to identify and being perfect in your answers. Miss so much as one stone and you fail. It's a standard I'd never before been required to meet in any previous educational pursuit, and it honestly scared the shit out of me.

I mean, *perfection*? How is that a realistic expectation? Especially for me, coming at this from outside the jewelry industry where the only gems I'd ever gotten my hands on were the ones I was examining in these courses.

My little studio on the Upper East Side didn't allow much room for a gemology laboratory, but I set up shop as best I could on the small desk in front of my bed. My microscope stood tallest, the outline of which I could study against the backdrop of the window on sleepless nights. A polariscope sat next to it, an eight-inch gadget whose lens indicated the optic character of a gem when looked through. The refractometer that sat nearby was especially beloved, only because I found the refractive indices of various gems to be the single most helpful clue to their eventual identification. If it looks like a ruby and shows a refractive index of 1.76, then nine times of out of ten, it's a ruby.

Next to these larger items sat a thick Ziploc bag in which I kept smaller things that the cat would fiddle with if left out. The spectrometer, like a doll-sized kaleidoscope, showed the spectrum of each gem when held against a bright and focused light source. I actually found this to be the most challenging tool to work with, in that no matter how hard I tried, the spectrums never showed up the way they did in the textbooks. The only one I could ever see clearly was garnet, which is why I loved when garnets showed up in my boxes of practice stones. Next to the spectrometer was a dichrometer, about the same size, that when looked through could show you if a gem contained multiple colors— two for dichroic and three for trichroic. The bag also contained a Chelsea filter, a small disk-like red lens that made certain gems appear certain colors, the most easy to use of all. Again, each of these devices yielded clues that could help with a gem's identification.

The bag also contained a polishing cloth, a bottle of super toxic refractive index fluid, and, my favorite piece of gemology equipment: my tweezers. These weren't tweezers like you'd buy off the shelf or for any of the elementary uses we've grown accustomed to associating with tweezers. These were diamond tweezers, meant for doing nothing but holding precious gems between the points. They were fabulous. They gave easily when pressed and had a sexy matte titanium finish.* I had put this particular pair of tweezers on my Christmas list the year before, and even just having cause to *put* gemological tweezers on my Christmas list delighted me. And every time I held up a gem to admire it, every time I rotated a stone under the microscope lens, every time I picked a gemstone up from the gem cloth on which I'd just polished it, I felt like a legitimate gemologist.

My gemology school would give me up to four boxes of stones at a time, each box corresponding to a particular assignment. The assignments were themed at first. A box focused on sapphire, then ruby. A box full of synthetic gems, then one with natural. A box of common yellow, orange, and gold stones. Then one of green. A box of stones containing phenomena. Then one with stones that were all opaque. As I progressed, the boxes became more random, which was my favorite. Not knowing what you were going to get, you could get anything. A synthetic opal triplet, followed by

---

*If it's wrong to use the word sexy to describe tweezers then I don't want to be right.

a rough piece of rhodochrosite, and then an emerald you could tell was natural by the presence of a whole host of messy inclusions.

There were special worksheets the school provided on which you were to work everything out. Gather evidence with your equipment and jot it all down as you went. I scribbled out countless copies of these worksheets from that little desk in my studio apartment, always in pencil, always with a few things erased and re-written multiple times.

These worksheets were pretty hardcore. There were more than twenty different things to be identified on each stone, and corresponding codes and letters and numbers to record for each. It was a science, a process. One that the institution swore by. I remember attending the class that taught me how to use all my gemology equipment and being completely skeptical about my ability to actually correctly identify a gemstone. I mean, what did *I* know about it? At the end of that particular course, we were each given a small box of five random gemstones and tasked with identifying them. I sat in paralyzed stillness for a moment, not sure what to do except begin working my way through the worksheet as I'd been taught. I took measurements, I made notes, and I ultimately identified four of the five stones correctly. I couldn't believe it. So the process *worked*.

And that's how I spent most of my days living in New York City. Sitting at my little desk filling out worksheets and identifying stones. Once I moved to Harlem and inherited a much larger desk from the previous tenant, my gem workspace became much more roomy. I could spread the worksheets out. I could fan the tiny gem-filled ziplocs as opposed to keep them all neatly pressed together in their box. I could have my thick textbook open as I flipped back and forth between topaz and tourmaline, which took me a little while to tell apart due to their refractive indices being so close.

Sure, I occasionally flipped a stone onto the floor and panicked I wouldn't find it before the cat did. Sure, I sometimes missed the FedEx man when he rang up with my new boxes of stones and then had to take the subway out to the Bronx to retrieve them at the sorting facility.* But other than that, it was idyllic. And when I think back on my life thus far, about stretches of time that simply delighted me, I can't think of anything that tops those months of studying gems. I had a whole city to explore, and I did, but what I loved most was returning home with a new box of stones, breaking the seal, and reaching for my tweezers as I turned on the microscope.

---

*If you ever want to feel like you are about to be murdered, walk back to the subway from the FedEx sorting facility in the Bronx, at night, with a backpack full of gems.

GOING

THE GOOD THING ABOUT PACKING UP YOUR furnished, 350-square-foot studio apartment is that it's very easy. None of the big stuff, like bed or dresser or table, comes with you. None of the little stuff, like towels or dishes or cleaning supplies, comes with you either. Truly, the only things needing transport to my new apartment some forty blocks uptown were my clothes, my cat, and my gemology equipment.

Cake.

Except not.

Because who wants to schlep *anything* forty Manhattan blocks?

Somehow even my few possessions ended up filling an entire car, a bright orange Pontiac that a friend offered for the endeavor. He and a few other volunteers helped bring boxes down the stairs, across the street, and into the Pontiac. The same group of friends then took the subway uptown and met us on the other end, the now-full Pontiac parked across the street from my new apartment. Everyone helped me unload, the process in reverse: boxes out of the car, across the street, and up the stairs.

It's a whole thing in Manhattan—moving people. Between various friends and acquaintances and the fleeting nature of leases and jobs and financial situations, there was always someone moving. The person would usually send out an email or put it on social media, an open invitation to help him move on a certain day and time. The mover offers promise of sustenance, maybe a few pizzas, and hopes for the best.

I participated in several of these moving out/moving in events, always made a bit tricky in that the volunteers have to get themselves from the old apartment to the new apartment, whatever vehicle being used for transporting the mover's possessions not having any leftover room to simultaneously transport volunteers. Once I got lucky and rode in the passenger seat of the large van my friend rented for her move, a few other people harbored in the back along with her small mountain of possessions.

On the unloading end of my move, I fed my volunteers macaroons from what until that morning had been my local bakery. They ate and wished me well in the new place, then disappeared into their days, a few of them hopping a ride in the now-empty Pontiac.

Alone in my new apartment, I peered out the only window into the morning sunshine. It's not so much that I was

Dorothy out of Kansas, because I'd only gone forty blocks. So how could there be so much difference between 78th Street and 119th?

Even in my initial explorations of this new part of town, there was quite obviously less money (cheaper rent being one of the core reasons why I'd moved there in the first place), a near complete lack of cute shops and bakeries, and most people out on the streets seemed to be loitering—standing around with groups of others, or even sitting in lawn chairs outside of buildings along the sidewalk, seemingly doing nothing—rather than purposefully going from point A to point B. Sometimes I wondered if I was being unfair to Harlem, feeling unsafe because everyone was black, or because everyone was standing around, or because there was no bakery with macaroons. Sometimes I wondered if people back home would believe me when I talked about how differently I now felt as I navigated the streets of my new neighborhood. Say what you will about bias and privilege, about me being unfair to Harlem, but never once while living on the Upper East Side did anyone show me their balls.

Struggling to fall asleep that first night as groups of people walked up and down the street, many yelling and hollering, I was completely on edge. I felt exposed, and, yes, unsafe. What were all these people even *doing* out in the middle of the night, anyway? And why were they yelling? Attempts at sleep eventually feeling futile, I flipped on the light and my eyes focused on a large dark spot on the floor. I grabbed my glasses, and the cockroach that came into focus struck me as infinitely worse and more threatening than anything going on outside in the street. I sat on the edge of my inflatable mattress, my tired heart full of panic, anger, and defeat. This was a mistake. The move was clearly a mistake.

Back at my old apartment the next morning to finish cleaning and hand over my keys, I yearned to stay. The memory of the previous night overwhelmed me as I stalled, unable to make myself get up from the chair in which I sat. Noise. Cockroach. Balls. Even with the bitch of a cat-hating woman below me, nothing seemed more important in that instant than never leaving that apartment. Never surrendering this address. Never subjecting myself to the debase horrors that awaited me forty blocks north. The slice of sun through the window warmed my chest and lap as I tightly hugged an armful of freshly-laundered towels. Here was safety. Here was warmth. Here was all the New York I knew.

But the towels did not belong to me. Nor did I inhabit this apartment as of that very morning. I stood up and strode to the door, locking it behind me. I caught a bus across town, a rather frustrating experience involving multiple unposted cancellations, and when I finally arrived at my Harlem apartment a couple of hours later, I thanked some unspoken transportation God that the west side would be so much easier to get around in.

And I guess that crappy bus ride is what started a change of thinking, because so what? So what if I was moving to a rather unglamorous part of the city? So what if I had to be more self-aware while walking home from the subway late at night? So what if I looked nothing like my neighbors? So what if there was one cockroach?* So what? So I would

---

*There were never any more, otherwise I would have had a big-ass problem.

find the bakeries and the pizza places. So I would embrace my new diverse surroundings. So I would decorate a new apartment. All while my cat was free to run around as much as she damn well pleased.

COMING

BEING UNEMPLOYED WHILE LIVING IN MANHAT~
tan is daunting even when it's part of your master plan and
your bank account is ridiculously padded. Indeed, I'd been
saving money for years and had more than enough to get me
through the completion of my gemology studies. And yet
somehow it's still hard to quell the panic that ensues when
you realize anything you spend will no longer automatically
be replenished in the form of bi-weekly direct deposits.

So when one of Pressure-Sensitive Leader's clients,
a label converter in Long Island, approached me about a
potential job opportunity, I couldn't help but be interested.

It didn't make sense, really. I mean, I'd chosen to leave
the label business. That was the whole point of this move; to
finish the gemology schooling that would take me years to

complete if I continued to give it nothing but the scraps of time I was rarely able to carve out of a schedule that included a full-time job. I had to get serious about the career shift I'd long been dreaming about. That I was even considering abandoning this plan in exchange for, well, a crap-ton of salary was pretty disgusting to me.

And yet I found myself agreeing to come out to Long Island for an interview.

A steady paycheck.

A Manhattan commute.

A company seeking me out.

All of these appealed to the logical, corporate part of me that wanted to feel valued and secure. They did nothing for the dreamer in me that craved a job I was more passionate about. But logic can be incredibly persuasive. So can money. And health insurance. So you can hardly blame me for hopping a train to Long Island.

I had a good relationship with one of this label converter's employees, a gentleman of about fifty who worked in their quality control department. I'd met him when I'd visited their offices in Long Island once before, at that time as an employee of Pressure-Sensitive Leader. I'd made the visit to present our new portfolio of custom labels, although what I remember from that day is not the presentation or how it went, but the fact that this quality control employee, who has since become a good friend of mine, greeted me with "I loved your book," marking the first time I'd ever come across a complete stranger who had read a book of mine. At that time I only had one book, but I couldn't get over how tickled I was to have found someone outside of my own circle of family and friends who had read it. Is this what real authors felt like?

Fast forward from that portfolio presentation to now, to me being an unemployed Manhattanite, and it was this same quality control employee who met me at the train station and drove us the short distance to the office. I can only describe what happened next as the best interview experience I have ever had. Like in my life.

Because I was everything they were looking for. And I heard this from each of my interviewers repeatedly. They were all men, as far as I can recall, and spread across various positions of importance within the organization. Each one shaking their heads in disbelief at how lucky it was that someone as perfect for their organization was now sitting in their conference room.

You're basically exactly what we're looking for.

That's exactly the skill set we would like to have.

That would be a huge help to our ability to win business.

This is everything we are looking for in this role.

A label converter spends its days printing labels, yes, but before those labels can be printed, the converter is fielding opportunities, bidding on projects, trying to secure additional pieces of business. As someone who had spent the better part of a decade working for the market leader in label materials, it made what I could offer this Long Island converter particularly valuable. Not only did I know our extensive selection of label materials and adhesives like the back of my hand, which would allow for better product recommendations and ultimately more business won for this label converter, but I had also spent several years working on optimizing the sizes and locations in which Pressure-Sensitive Leader offered those label materials. That meant I could save this company money as I purposely selected the combinations of materials that would best work in their—and their customers'—favor. My quality control friend took me to lunch after the interviews, echoing the positive sentiment I'd heard all morning. I was a perfect fit. Somehow the topic of salary came up as we dined, although in the unofficial way with which friends speak about such things. I had no idea how much a job like this in this in a place like this might pay, and I probably said as much.

"You made six figures at Pressure-Sensitive Leader, right?" he asked me.

"Yes," I answered. "Would this job be six figures?"

"I would assume mid," he replied, which I interpreted as my friend assuming that the job I had just crushed the interviews for was going to pay somewhere between $140,000 and $160,000.

It was all I could do not to drop my fork. Or gape, open-mouthed.

Because that was significantly more than I had been making at Pressure-Sensitive Leader, and although it would be the very definition of selling out, in my then-current state of unemployment, I knew that if they offered me this job at that salary, I would take it.

As I corresponded with my interviewers over the coming days, chiefly the company's owner, the only place where things got sticky was when it came to my desire to reside in Manhattan. It's not *that* far, right? Except that it was. Certainly when it came to the commute. Even just getting to their office for the interviews had taken a staggering two-and-a-half hours. And that was just one way. It involved first walking from my apartment to the Lexington and 77th Street subway station, a distance of almost half a mile. Then catching the subway downtown to Penn Station. Then taking a train to the Long Island Rail Road station. Then a whole separate train out to Long Island. And finally a short walk from the train station to the office. All of which could be made more lengthy depending on train times, delays, and weather. Was I really willing to spend five hours of every weekday commuting? Even for that amount of money?

Of course I discussed a number of options with the company's owner. There had been times, he explained, when they'd rented a local apartment there on Long Island for employees who lived in Manhattan. We discussed having me live in a rented apartment in Long Island for an initial period of training, then commuting from Manhattan after that. We discussed having me stay in the rented apartment in Long Island a few days a week, working remotely from Manhattan all the others. We discussed me continuing to live in Manhattan but make the commute to Long Island only every other day. We discussed many iterations of these types of arrangements, but the bottom line was this: if they were going to be paying me this much, they wanted me in Long Island. And it was at this point that I was able to shake myself free of the pursuit of the security that such a salary would bring.

Because what good would it do me to have moved to New York only to continue in the same lackluster industry? How would a 2.5-hour-each-way commute not completely suck my will to live? How could I abandon the Manhattan that for years had enticed me to its gridded city blocks? Most importantly, how would I get closer to my gemology dream by not focusing full time on my studies?

It reminds me of that poem, the one by Langston Hughes. Because what *does* happen to a dream deferred? Does it become a raisin in the sun? A festering sore? I'm sure it can take many forms, one of which is undoubtedly a handsome salary bulleting across the Long Island Rail Road at dawn.

Sidebar: Temperature Control and an Illustration of the Robustness of my Paranoia

For most Americans, temperature control in our homes is a thing. In that we have the ability to cool or heat our homes with the simple push of a button or turn of a dial. This usually involves vents, sometimes ceiling heat, and it's nothing short of a modern miracle.

The first home I lived in after finishing college and graduate school was a boxy, two-story charmer in East Cleveland. I loved the house fiercely, down to the different colors of paint in each room and the small hexagonal window in the master bedroom closet. My only complaint was how difficult and expensive it was to heat. Cleveland winters were unlike anything I'd ever experienced, and the months of October through May required near constant heat.

I made several blunders during my years in Cleveland, including turning off the heat completely in December while out of town for my brother's wedding. My first winter there, and I was more concerned about paying for heat I wouldn't be using than I was about making sure the pipes didn't freeze. I confess it had never occurred to me that they could freeze at all. It happened twice, both times shocking as I went to turn on the faucet to find nothing flowing. Equally shocking was that the plumber's remedy involved a blow dryer and a strategically placed overnight space heater. Even *I* could have thought of that.

The heat in my Cleveland house was perpetually on, the gas firing every few minutes as the temperature inside dipped below my desired setting. The frustrating thing was that the only times the house felt warm were when the heat was actually coming out of the vents. As soon as it stopped, the house would feel cold and drafty. You pretty much had to be standing directly in front of a vent while the heat was coming out in order to be warm. I had a vent right next to my bed, one right next to the couch, and one by the toilet, so most of the time I was fine, but this kind of fine still necessitated the constant wearing of a thick, fuzzy bathrobe and made me dread the seconds between getting out of bed in the morning and putting on said thick, fuzzy bathrobe.

Unlike my Cleveland house, my studio apartment in New York City didn't have vents. Like almost all the old walk-up buildings in New York, it had a radiator affixed to one wall; a painted, hissing thing that was simply so hot that it radiated warmth throughout the apartment. Which is not hard to do when your apartment is a single rectangular room. The other thing about heating my New York apartment was that unlike Cleveland, I wasn't actually able to control it at all. I couldn't make the radiator come on more or less often, or hiss hotter or cooler. I was stuck with whatever temperature the basement boiler was set to churn out.

I thought about this a lot. *The boiler.* I had no idea what to picture when envisioning this massive heating mechanism that warmed our whole building. My only experience with the term had been the single season of *My So-Called Life*, where many key scenes between Claire Danes and Jared Leto take place in "the boiler room."

From what I gathered, the boiler must have been set to overdrive, because the temperature in my New York apartment was almost always stiflingly hot. I took to propping the lone window open with a small wooden block, a block I rarely removed, even in winter. Not an ideal solution, as I was constantly worried that my small cat would wriggle herself through the opening and onto the fire escape, maybe down to the courtyard even. Or more worried still that the bitchy downstairs neighbor who hated the cat would use the open window to get in and off the cat while I wasn't home. Or, more realistically since she was in her seventies and relatively frail, that she would hire someone to do it for her. And yes, these are actual thoughts that I actually had. All the time. To the point that I would remove the block and close the window when paranoia got the better of me, only to open it again when the apartment got so hot that it felt like a form of torture. *I'LL TELL YOU ANYTHING YOU WANT TO KNOW!*

At some point in the year, either late winter or early spring, there was a noticeable decrease in the building temperature. If I recall correctly, there had been some sort of outage. And the outage had somehow messed with the boiler, in that I think my landlords had tried to put it back to the correct setting, only they couldn't remember exactly what that setting had been.

The cooler apartment temperature was the best thing

that had happened since I moved in. Every day just felt so *refreshing*. No more constant need to prop open the window. No more constant exposure to potential cat burglars. I assumed everyone in the building must be feeling the same relief, but then a neighbor knocked on my door.

This woman's apartment was next to mine, ours being the back, courtyard-facing apartments on the third floor. She had a loud voice and sounded like a New Yorker. She worked from home and watched a lot of TV, and now here she was on the other side of my door, a scarf wrapped around her neck and a stocking cap on her head.

Um, was she living in the same building I was?

"I was just wondering," she began, "if you've noticed it's a lot colder in the building lately."

Cold is not exactly how I would have described it. It's more like things used to be stifling and now they were a temperature people might actually choose to live in. Still, it was colder than it had been, and, yes, I had noticed.

"The temperature is cooler, yes," I answered.

"Well, don't you think it's *freezing*?" she asked, rubbing her shoulders and then wrapping her scarf more tightly around her neck.

"It's cooler, yes," I said, not wanting to admit that I thought the new temperature was perfect.

"Well, since you have an in with them," meaning my landlords, "can you ask if they can turn the boiler up?"

I felt bad for lying, for assuring her I would, but I just couldn't go back to the old temperature. I couldn't give up this ground I'd won, by sheer luck and a power outage. I didn't want anything touching that boiler. Unless it was Jared Leto.

COMING

SO MAYBE RE~EMPLOYING MYSELF IN THE LABEL
business didn't make sense. Maybe having a full-time job
didn't either. But what if I could find a way to work out a
part-time gig, and one that was within the jewelry industry?
Wouldn't that both quell the financial panic I was always
trying to beat off with a stick *and* get me a foot in the door
within the industry I had my eye on? Aren't I just *so* smart?

Over the years I confess I'd occasionally surfed the
Tiffany & Co. website. I made no secret in my second book
that working at Tiffany would in many ways be a dream job
for me; one I'd drop everything for if ever I was to be given
an opportunity. But an opportunity is exactly the thing they
had never given me. Not that I'd tried very hard, aside from
sending a few mediocre resumes full of labels and logistics

and impressive stats about increased adhesive technology sales. I always felt simultaneously excited and humiliated when I pictured my profile being viewed by a gaggle of Tiffany HR employees. Or, more likely, one.

On one hand, maybe they'd call me. Maybe they'd be impressed with my accomplishments, my education, my mad love for their company. Maybe I was just who they were looking for. On the other hand, there was nothing gemmy about me on paper. Nothing that identified me as someone fit for a career at the most iconic luxury jewelry brand. Not surprisingly, none of my feeble attempts ever garnered a response.

But perhaps actually living in New York gave me a better shot at being considered. If they didn't have to fly me in, perhaps it was worth bringing me in for an interview. Of course, this still left the issue of time, in that I really wasn't looking for full-time employment. I had to study. I had to become a gemologist.

The stars aligned when a part-time internship opened up in Tiffany's marketing department. And suddenly I wondered if I'd been going about this all wrong. Tiffany likely hadn't been interested in me because my by-now solid history of work experience left me seeking jobs that were not entry level. Yet without knowing me, and without any jewelry history or experience on my resume, they weren't willing to give me anything *above* entry level. So what if I took the internship, giving them the chance to see me, get to know me, learn how ridiculously dedicated I was to their brand? What if I proved myself and the internship then led to a full-time job just when I finished my gemology studies? So smart.

I was shocked when the plan worked, insofar as someone from Tiffany's HR department responded to my resume and cover letter and I ended up with an interview scheduled for the following week. To think that after all that time, all it took was being willing to take a menial position at very low pay. Honestly, they'd be getting such a steal. I'd take my extra decade of experience and my MBA-level insights and my life-long passion for the brand and blow the bejeezus off of any intern they'd ever had before.

And I'd like to pause here, letting us all bask in this euphoria of opportunity and excitement. Think of how it would feel to be given an opportunity to interview with your dream company. I looked at the email confirming my interview time and location over and over again, a pulse of anxiety and glee rushing through me each time I paused my gaze over the Tiffany logo at the top of the screen. I imagined the words I would use to announce that I'd been hired by the company where I'd most wanted to work. The world was my pearl-bearing oyster.

I wore multiple pieces of Tiffany jewelry to the interview, twisting my bracelet nervously as the lady at the desk in the lobby checked me in. I hadn't known that most corporate Tiffany positions work out of a building in the Flatiron district, quite a jaunt from the flagship store. I was escorted up to a small conference room where I was interviewed by two women concurrently. Both middle-aged and pleasant, we discussed my background, my experience, and their confusion over why someone in my situation would want an internship. And in what I thought was a winningly honest answer, I explained how I was completely willing to do what it took to get my foot in the door and prove myself at the company I had for so long admired.

Returning home after the interview, I immediately fired off the obligatory thank you emails to my interviewers, a must in the world of business, and was quite shocked to never hear back. Not just from these women, who perhaps hadn't seen the point of replying to a thank you email, or perhaps had disliked me greatly, but also from HR. From anyone. No one ever reached out to tell me yes or no. It's ghosting, corporate style, and it's very inappropriate.

I flashed back to my first year in business school when Theme Park Giant had shattered my illusion of their monopoly on happiness by not only offering me a piss-poor salary for an internship, but by then making it clear that they didn't care whether or not I accepted, as they could get a hundred girls to take my place. Everyone wanted to work for Theme Park Giant. Everyone likewise wanted to work for Tiffany, this epitome of jewelry dreams, part blue box and part Hepburn. So they certainly didn't need to tiptoe around my feelings, or really make any effort to behave the way a company does when it needs to get people to like them, to want them, to apply for their jobs.

It was upsetting to me at the time, the lack of common courtesy as well as the apparent impossibility of me ever being what they were looking for, but I've made peace with it. I still visit their stores and smile, I still wear my Tiffany pieces with pride, and I still send thank you notes after interviews. My mama raised me right.

Those bitches.

GOING

SO TIFFANY WAS A BUST, BUT IT STILL SEEMED like I was onto something with the idea of a part-time job within the jewelry industry. Thinking something less corporate might be the ticket, I began looking for jobs that combined writing with jewelry, maybe something I could do from home as I completed gemology assignments and explored the city.

When I saw a posting for a job writing descriptions for a jewelry catalog, it struck me as ideal. Because if there's one thing on which I could infinitely wax prolific, it was describing jewelry.

The man hiring for the position, Arnie, liked that my background included both writing and gemology classes and asked me to send over some sample descriptions for a few pictures he emailed me, each of a relatively decadent piece of jewelry. Not knowing what character or word limits might be in place for this particular publication, and encouraged by Arnie's invitation to "be creative," I went all out.

This stunning pear-shaped pendant features two loops of identically-sized melee diamonds. The circles of melee that connect the loops contain center-stone diamonds that increase in size down the length of the pendant. The two almost brooch-like embellishments, one connecting the pendant to its chain and the other sitting atop the pear's point, provide dimension and a heightened sense of glamour.

This 'Star Within a Star' pendant features pave-style melee diamonds elegantly set in platinum. Each of the ten petals on the star flowers is unique and imperfectly shaped, a nod to the patterns typically found in nature, and the multiple layers, complete with four crowning diamonds on top, create a three-dimensional effect that admirers will want to get a closer look at.

This beautiful pendant features alternating swirls of black and colorless diamonds. A very modern setting, featured here in 18K white gold, the pave-style arrangement of the diamonds minimizes the appearance of prongs and enhances sparkle from any direction, and the two-tone diamond color compliments all skin tones and background colors.

To be fair, these kind of suck. And in the first example, I had to actually dig through my emails and look back at the picture as I was writing this book to see what the hell I was even talking about. *Circles of melee that connect the loops?* Whatever. The point is, words came easy to me, and it seemed like writing jewelry descriptions was something one could do while basically rearranging the same set of basic jewelry vocabulary into different patterns. And if someone was going to pay me a decent hourly rate to crank these out, I could certainly oblige. Again, not that I was in dire financial straits. I just knew I'd feel better about attending Broadway shows and eating Carnegie Deli cheesecake if I were at least earning a bit of spending money.

"Looks good," Arnie said when he read my descriptions. "Also, just out of curiosity, are you proficient in digital marketing, considering that you have a writing background?"

Not an entirely specific question, in that "proficient" and "digital marketing" probably fall on a spectrum of inter-pretation, but I did tell Arnie that I had a lot of experience writing pieces and articles for websites and blogs.

"Would you be interested in writing blogs for us on jewelry trends, diamonds, and gemstones?" Arnie asked. "We can pay you $30 per blog, and you can write up to ten blogs per week."

In truth, I was less excited about writing blogs than I was about writing jewelry descriptions, in that blogs take more time and more brain power, but once Arnie knew I had experience with blogs, it became his only offer. He even told me the jewelry descriptions job was no longer available. I felt somewhat cornered, a hint of bait and switch, but I did want the gig. The only issue for me became the money, which seemed much too little.

"I'm certainly interested in blogging, but considering how many hours it would take, not to mention the research that would need to go into it, I could not afford to do it for $30 per blog," I replied.

I asked for $75, to which Arnie said he would need to see a writing sample, which I happily supplied that very day. The phone conversation that followed is one I wish I had recorded, because Arnie not only agreed to increase the pay, but also admitted the reason was because my writing had "swagger."

His word, not mine.

Swagger.

It's a little thing, really, but I've held onto this word in the years since Arnie used it to describe my writing. I pull it out and look at it when I'm feeling down about being a writer who nobody reads. I dust it off when I need to know that the way I string my words together is different than the ways most other people do. I say it out loud when I need a reminder of why it is that I do this.

And so I took my swagger and started writing blogs for Arnie and his diamond company, usually on a list of topics he supplied, occasionally on a list of topics of my own choosing. The good news was I soon discovered that writing jewelry blogs contains a lot of the same rearrangement of basic jewelry content that writing jewelry descriptions does, and it took a surprisingly little amount of time to crank out my weekly 8-10 blogs.

Arnie's company had an office in the diamond district on

47th Street, but we managed to get by with phone and email correspondence. Things functioned remarkably well, me submitting my blogs and him mailing a check each week. And it seemed like I'd hit the remarkable sweet spot that is freelance writing. It wasn't enough to pay my rent, I didn't have healthcare, and sometimes I worried all these blogs were going to come back and haunt me if I ended up with a big job within the gemology industry—or *any* job within the gemology industry—but it finally felt like I'd found the ideal way to keep some money coming in while I remained unemployed during my studies.

Several months later, after I'd accepted a position with a gem institute that I couldn't believe I'd been lucky enough to get, I told Arnie I'd need to stop blogging. Not only because I wouldn't have the time, but I also half suspected it might now be a conflict of interest for me to be spouting a bunch of jewelry and gemology content. Why, I'd written blogs for Arnie on the benefits of buying a lab-grown diamond, the benefits of buying a diamond online, the totally not-a-big-dealness of a diamond that has been enhanced, none of which are things I personally believe in. Like at all.

I went into Arnie's office on 47th Street to collect my final check and say goodbye, and while I'm sure he wished me well, he did his best to convince me to reconsider.

"We're going to have a lot more writing and blogging coming up. It would be a great opportunity for you, and a lot more money."

What I wanted to tell Arnie was that unless he could pay me six figures, there was no way I was turning down the gem institute, but what struck me in that instant was that if he *could* have matched the gem institute's offer, I would have said yes. All things being equal, I would have preferred to stay in that studio apartment, writing blogs at my leisure, occasionally glancing out the window at the kids running up and down the stairs of the brownstone across the street, breaking at lunch for a quick walk through Central Park. Nice work if you can get it.

Sidebar: Dating in the City and How Cologne Has Ruined Me

I'd always heard that Manhattan was a singles hotspot; that along with Boston and D.C., it's one of the best cities to live in if dating is high on your priority list. It's estimated that 60 percent of the population in New York City is single, creating what seems like an obvious hotbed of budding relationships.

Of course, what the stats *don't* tell you is that there are some dating mismatches that have resulted in a surplus of what is most definitely *not* dating. The most compelling case I've found is the argument that over the course of time, college-educated women have come to far outnumber college-educated men, meaning a woman wishing to find a man who is on par with her—on everything from income potential to intellectual capacity—has far fewer options than do the men. She has to either beat out a number of

other women to win a man's affection, or she has to settle for someone without a college education. But more challenging even than competition is that a woman must then convince a man to give up his position as a limited and desirable commodity and commit to her rather than continue to be a limited and desirable commodity.

Right.

It's the Golden Cock Syndrome at its finest. A man is demotivated from pairing off when the alternative leaves him free to be the object of so much desire. When there aren't enough men to go around, the surplus of women creates a perfect scenario for single men. I mean, why would they give that up by becoming *not* single?

This is all to say that I didn't see much dating going on in New York. Even at *church*, which is how I met most of the men I knew, the men weren't dating. *Did you hear what I said?* Not even *church men* were dating! Men who'd been raised on the "marriage and family" line their whole lives. And it wasn't just that they weren't dating *me*. They weren't dating anyone. It was all rather odd.

The most time I ever spent with a potential suitor while living in New York didn't even come from an organic city-ish meet cute. He wasn't even a New Yorker. He wasn't even an American. A woman I'd known in Cleveland wanted to set me up with her brother-in-law, who drove down from Toronto for a long weekend to meet me. He rented an Airbnb a few blocks away, and when we met up at Serendipity—my suggestion—I was hopeful. His mop of pleasant brown hair, his easy laugh, his dorky glasses. I kind of liked him.

Things deteriorated quickly, mostly because four days is

too long to spend with someone you're just meeting, even when he's not staying under your roof. It was too drawn out, too forced, too much time for him to fill space with questions like, "If you were a color, what would you be?" I honestly couldn't wait for him to leave and probably didn't do a very good job of concealing that. I've never spoken to the Cleveland woman again, mostly because I'm embarrassed of what he probably told her about me. At one point, I may or may not have lost my temper in the middle of Times Square when he wouldn't stop trying to grab hold of me and guide me through the busy streets. The streets I *lived on and managed to successfully navigate—by myself—every day.* It was all just too much.

I do remember another man, a New Yorker, who called me up and asked me out, a surprising gesture in this era of Golden Cocks and texting. It was a man I unfortunately wasn't interested in for a variety of reasons. Namely he was shorter and skinnier than I was—both hard to accomplish—and wore such heavy cologne that it actually impaired my ability to function. I considered asking him to wear less but couldn't work up the nerve. Of course, none of this really matters because if a man's going to call me up and ask me out, I'm going to say yes. Call it encouraging good behavior, call it rare, call it simply the right thing to do, but I figure everyone deserves a date.

He took me to the Met, as, shockingly, I had not yet been. Truth be told, I'm not a huge museum enthusiast, mostly because I'm just not interested enough to stay very long. I like to go in and see the things I want to see, but in relatively short order I'm usually ready to leave and go get a snack. Mr. Cologne was an excellent guide, expertly explaining paintings as we made our way through the various wings. My biggest fear was that he'd insist we go through the entire museum, or that I'd pass out from the cologne-induced headache I'd been battling since we arrived.

But just then we entered a new room, and I brightened. Because on the wall directly in front of me was the painting that had hung on the living room wall of my childhood home. And how was this possible? The painting—a woman seated at a piano, a girl standing next to her holding a violin, and another watching both of them rather wistfully—was one I had studied so many times growing up. I liked to pretend that it was us. My mom sitting at the piano, my sister with the violin, and me, the littlest, watching and maybe singing along. I had loved this painting fiercely yet had no idea that it was an *actual painting*. A famous one. A Renoir.

I asked my date to take my picture next to it, still unable to believe my luck at coming across this particular painting in this particular wing. Things improved further when a few minutes later I witnessed a man kneel down in front of his girlfriend, the painting behind him full of white flowers, hints of orange and yellow at the center of each blossom, and ask her to marry him. They were smiling, people ogling from across the room, trying to give the couple their privacy but also trying desperately to be a part of it all. She said yes and they embraced, the white flowers so beautiful behind them. I wondered if he'd picked this painting specifically.

We left the museum, my fragrant date and I, me feeling uplifted by the Renoir and downright delighted over the proposal. At least *someone* in this city wanted to settle down. And I'll bet he wore almost no cologne.

GOING

THERE USED TO BE A MUSEUM IN TIMES SQUARE —some ingeniously creative name like The Times Square Museum or the Museum of Times Square—that I loved to visit. Even before I moved to New York, I'd make the pilgrimage to this museum every time I was in town. Small and on the whole rather underwhelming—there was no admission fee—the museum contained artifacts relevant to those crowded, colorful streets. Things like costumes worn in Broadway plays, various photos and plaques, even a replica of the giant ball that drops just before midnight on New Year's Eve.

The ball was particularly captivating. Because it's hard to beat that moment. We get it each year, but no other single moment feels as significant. The year is over. It's spent. The things you didn't accomplish and the keeper of a man you didn't meet combine with the potential of these things happening in the new year. Together they create a hope so palpable it literally moves you off your feet as the ball begins to drop. It has you counting down under your breath. It has you fixed on the ball, growing ever closer to its midnight goal, and wishing for the thing you want most as the year switches over.

Which brings me to what was my favorite thing in the Times Square museum, the wishing wall.

It took me a minute to comprehend what it was the first time I saw it. Because at first glance, it just looked like a colorful wall of paper squares, held up with thumb tacks and each containing a hand-written wish made by someone who'd visited the museum. Not unlike similar walls at other museums that are trying to introduce a personalized, interactive component. Even the Museum of Ice Cream has a wall where you can eek out messages in pink magnetic letters.

I would have participated anyway, but once I actually read the explanatory plaque next to the wall, I learned that these very squares of colorful tissue paper were collected from this wall and used as the confetti that came raining down from the sky at the stroke of midnight on New Year's Eve. And this changed *everything*. Because you know how I feel about New Year's Eve. And to think that the dreams and hopes and wishes—yours bundled together with thousands of others—were what filled the sky in that moment gave me a feeling I couldn't really place. It wasn't sentimentality. There's nothing particularly sentimental about dreams. It was hopeful, yes, but also very real. In that these were actual things. That actual people had actually written. And this opened the possibility for someone to see *my* confetti square as it fell, to pick it up off of the pavement and read it, to wonder about the person who had scrawled those few words with the utmost sincerity.

I suppose when you got right down to it, what this all made me feel was *connected.* Connected to all the other wish-makers, strangers to me, except not really—we are all alike in our wanting. Connected to the universe after putting into words the thing I most desired of it. And connected to myself for being able to pinpoint this desire in the first place.

Most years, the wish I wrote on my confetti square when visiting the museum had something to do with love, a common theme when reading along the wall. It is, after all, universally coveted. In looking back over the years of wishes on the Times Square museum wall, I can actually gauge time by the state of my heart. One year I wished that the man who'd just broken mine would change his mind and marry me. The next year I wished to meet someone new. And the year after that I wished to just be happy even if I never met *anyone.* None of these came true in those particular years, which could prove that this is all complete crap. But it still felt immensely important to scribble out my wish for each year on that little square of colored tissue. Even if my wishes were trivial compared to those asking for cancer to be cured, for relatives to stop being abusive, for that long-desired baby.

Toward the end of the December of my first winter living in New York, I began debating whether or not I should go to Times Square to see the ball drop for myself. I wasn't really going for the ball drop, of course, or for Ryan Seacrest, or for the thermos of hot chocolate I would take with me. I was going for those confetti squares. But going brought up all kinds of annoying challenges, chief among them being the unbearably bitter cold, even with hot chocolate. Not to mention the number of hours I'd have to be there in order to secure a place in the crowd. I mean, how were these people even going to the bathroom?

I threw the idea out to a few friends just to see if anyone would bite, but they all groaned and rolled their eyes. No New Yorker actually *wanted* to go to Times Square on New Year's Eve. That was for tourists, they told me. That was hell.

Still undecided, I took the subway over to Times Square the night before the festivities, so December 30. It was late, it was cold, but the place was still hopping. The stage was set up, Ryan Seacrest in the midst of a rehearsal. There were so many people standing under the ball taking pictures that in the one I took, it actually looks—from all the other arms with cameras taking the exact same shot—like it was New Year's Eve. It looks like midnight. It looks like The Moment.

I'm ashamed to admit that I posted this picture the following night, on New Year's Eve, just after midnight, even though what I'd done that evening was go to a movie by myself and then watch the ball drop from the little TV in my apartment. The picture is misleading, but it just seemed like something I should be doing. It seemed like where I should have been. Where I wanted people to think I was. Knowing I'd have to be there for all that time by myself had been the kicker; the thing I couldn't get past. But why did anyone else have to know that?

And so I've never seen it live. I've only imagined what it

must be like to watch all those paper squares flutter down, rotating over and then over again, moving with the wind, with the momentary heat of celebration. It's a comfort to me that some of those wishes come true. Some people get their paper square dreams. Because some people *do* beat cancer. Some *do* break free from their abusers. Some babies *do* get born to those who want them most. And even if you've never been one of these people, even if you've never been so lucky, even if it's a complete crapshoot and your square will likely fall to the universe's ground unnoticed, why not at least put yourself in the running?

Of course, for those who were fooled by my faux New Year's Eve picture, there was a dead giveaway that would have clued them in. There's a reason why it's not and will never be the picture I wanted.

There is no confetti.

COMING

THE SITUATION WITH MY DOWNSTAIRS NEIGH~
bor didn't get any better. It got worse. Or maybe what got
worse was how badly I handled it. This woman became the
bane of my existence. And I began to dread being at my
apartment. Which was kind of a problem, seeing as how I
lived there. I didn't even have a 9:00 to 5:00 job that took
me elsewhere.

I'd start the day feeling peaceful and happy as I looked
over at my sleeping cat curled on the foot of the bed. There was
so much to love about my current situation. Not having a day
job is wonderful enough—sleeping in, wearing pajamas, no
commute—but not having a day job in New York City is particularly delightful. Where else are you mere steps away from any
number of daytime errands—the post office, the library, the

grocery store, the dry cleaner, the gym. Where else can you pop over to Central Park at 3:00 just because you want to?

But these reveries of contentment fell to pieces the moment my cat stirred and gave any sign that she was about to jump down and move about the floor. I learned to dread my cat being awake, all because of the inevitable scolding from the woman downstairs.

Someone with a stronger constitution could have handled it better, surely, but I lived in fear of the brooming and the obscenities. I lived with the single objective to keep my cat as still as possible. I even resorted to shutting my cat in the bathroom overnight to prevent her from running around while I slept. No easy task, as I had to jerry-rig the door shut in such a way that she couldn't open it. And then there was the crippling guilt from the occasional meow that would echo from behind the door.

It was easy to boil this all down to the woman downstairs being a total bitch, because she seemed the very personification of one. It became less easy when I found out she was in her seventies and battling cancer. "Poor woman," some said, or, "She always feels so sick and cranky from the chemo," or, "Hearing a jungle tiger cat above her is really the last thing she needs." (OK, that last one I made up.)

I did feel badly for her, but was it really a sufficient excuse to harass me, particularly for having a small, quiet pet that I was totally allowed to have? What I'm trying to say is that despite her age and ailing health, I was never able to see her as anything other than a bitch. I may burn in hell for that, but it's the principle of the thing. And some things you just can't let go.

In the course of complaining to my landlord about all this cat harassing, I found out that this woman had worked in some sort of government capacity but had been on disability for decades. So she was home all day, too. She'd lived in her apartment for so long that she paid something ridiculous like $150 in controlled rent and so would never leave. Her apartment was so messy and full of crap that the building had, before my time, once had a vermin problem that originated from her. And she'd never had anyone above her who'd had a pet, so no one had known she would react in this particular way.

Still, I couldn't help feeling a bit duped. That whole time I'd looked at the place and signed the contract, prepared to move, and then lugged my suitcases up the stairs and got settled and met the other tenants and no one bothered to mention the bitch who lived below me? Had I purposely been tricked so my landlord could pocket the handsome monthly rent?*

The apartment building was run by a co-op, my landlord being a big part of the co-op leadership, and apparently everyone on the board was well aware of the problem this woman posed. Everyone was aware of how difficult she was, how unpleasant, how abusive. Other tenants began apologizing to me in hushed tones when we'd meet in the stairwell. But I didn't really want their pity. I wanted them to take action. I wanted the co-op board to kick her sorry cancerous ass out into the street. I wanted her gone.

The board did craft a series of mildly threatening letters

---

*I do not actually think this was the case, but in the moment, I was grasping at blame straws.

in which they told the woman she had to behave better, specifically to me. That action would be taken if she didn't. She basically laughed in their faces and said she and her lawyer would fight tooth and nail to stay; that she had every right to voice her discontent for the disturbance that the jungle tiger cat upstairs caused to her and her health. So the board never made good on any threat. They told me there was really nothing they could do. And the brooming and yelling continued.

My landlord did install additional carpet in my apartment in an effort to muffle the sound. It didn't seem to lessen my downstairs neighbor's annoyance, or the frequency with which she hassled me. And despite my single solitary outburst where I made as much noise as possible simply to piss her off, I'm just not cut out for battles with people who can continue to make life worse for me if they choose. So I adopted a resolve to be as rational and kind as I could to this woman, never wanting to give her any real reason to complain about me. Somehow knowing that the only complaint she had, the jungle tiger cat, was completely irrational made me feel like I had the logical and moral high ground.

This downstairs neighbor did her shopping late at night, a fact I learned when arriving home from a trip at some ungodly hour and being surprised to find her wheeling her small shopping basket (the one many New Yorkers keep outside their apartment doors for use when fetching groceries) into the building's entryway. She stopped to check her mail, as did I, and it was odd to be in such close proximity to this woman who was so awful to me.

Did she know I was the one with the cat?

As the newest of only sixteen tenants in the building, I figured she must. Tapping into my reserve of moral high ground, I spoke first.

"Hi. I live upstairs from you. I'm just getting back from a trip, and my cat tends to run a round a lot when she's excited that I've come home. So I just want to let you know that she might make more noise than usual tonight."

This woman, short and a bit stout, a handkerchief tied over her bald head, looked up at me with eyes that looked every bit like I'd just given her the moon.

"Thank you so much," she began, very sincerely. "To be given a heads up like that, that's really all I ask, and that was very thoughtful of you."

I couldn't believe the exchange had gone so well. I was almost giddy as I unpacked my suitcase, cat running around excitedly, to the sound of silence downstairs. So this is what it had been like. To exist in one's own home in a state completely free of stress. And to think that one exchange was all it took to turn things around!

The brooming and shouting was back within a few hours—so much for a truce—but for those brief shining moments, I remembered what it was like to be unfettered from other people's crazy.

GOING

TO EXPLAIN HOW I CAME TO BE STANDING IN front of the Rockefeller Center Christmas tree at 5:30 in the morning and soaking wet, I'll need to give you a bit of backstory.

See, I can't actually say that I've experienced Christmas in New York. Aside from the year I went to Paris for the holiday, I've spent every Christmas of my life with family. So there was never a question of whether I would go home for Christmas once I moved to New York. I would, obviously, which means all I can really say is that I've experienced *Christmastime* in New York.

Granted, it's not a Notre Dame Cathedral mass, nor is it the Christmas Eve choir of nuns at the Sacré-Coeur. It's not the towering red tree inside the Paris Opera House, and it's not the one inside the Galleries Lafayette either. It's not even the small, cheese-filled Christmas markets set up in various neighborhoods, or the big one along the Champs Élyssées. Indeed, once you've experienced Christmas in Paris, what chance does any other city really have? But that said, December in New York City is not without magic.

A good portion of that magic is the lights and decorations in and outside of stores and shops, everything from little corner bakeries to the cascading strands down the side of Bloomingdales. It seemed like every establishment I passed made me want to go in. Christmas shopping then became a particular treat—taking the subway to my favorite stores with a certain gift in mind and walking out with boxes wrapped in sharply creased paper and tied with festive ribbon. I selected chocolates for my mom, flavored olive oil for my dad, a book for my nephews. I could have gone into every shop in the entire city if I'd had the time and money.

My favorite store at the holidays was Tiffany & Co. To be fair, it was my favorite store regardless of the season and I visited often. Always a special place for me—almost no one uses as highly-graded diamonds in their jewelry—it was spectacular dressed in its holiday décor. My favorite were the wreaths that hung on every crevice, above every stairwell. They were a mix of green and gold, but mostly they were a vision in Tiffany blue from a combination of ribbons and box-shaped ornaments. I loved that such a non-holiday color still got top billing within its walls.

Another reason Christmastime in New York City is so magical is that many of the nationally celebrated events that ring in the season happen there. From the Thanksgiving Day parade that ends with Santa's debut to the lighting of the tree at Rockefeller Center, so many eyes are on New York.

The tree was of particular fascination to me as a newcomer, mostly because I'd never before seen it in real life. Was it as big as it looked on TV? Could you take a picture with the tree in its entirety? You could, it turned out, but a shot from the "official" photo spot—the absolute best view of the tree, mind you—meant waiting in line along with the throngs of mostly tourists who were hanging around seeking out such things.

The whole square there was crowded during the holidays, people ice skating or shopping or waiting for their turn for pictures with the tree, making it one of the last places you'd want to be. Yet I *did* want to be there. I wanted to see the tree, to bask in its greatness. And silly as this made me, I wanted that damn photo.

What you might not know about the tree in Rockefeller Center—and what I certainly didn't until doing a little bit of research—is that they turn the lights on at 5:30 in the morning. And in case they are escaping you, let me remind you of the three best things about New York City in December at 5:30 in the morning.

1. It's still dark as night outside.
2. No one is around.
3. The photo-op spot is unmanned.

This lights-on time is some pretty valuable intel. And if you live in or are vacationing in Manhattan in December, this is hands down the best way to get your photo with the Rockefeller Center tree.

The trouble with the morning I selected for my photo-op was that it was pouring rain. I'd recruited a few friends to join me and was waiting under the doorway of the Rockefeller building since I had arrived first. I had an umbrella, but this was serious rain. In the realm of what you might call torrential. I wished my friends would hurry up, worried the security guard pacing a short distance away would at some point tell me I couldn't just use Rockefeller Center as a shield from the rain. Would he think I was homeless?

The lights had by this time been turned on, and from my vantage point—basically right under it—the tree was spectacular. So, to once again bring you up to speed on where we are, this is me, getting the entire Rockefeller Center tree to myself.

It was big but not so big that you couldn't take it in. And it was bright but surprisingly simple in theme. I remember the lights as nearly all white, because that's how they look in the photo I took, nothing like the traditional colored strands you see on the trees and houses in your own neighborhood. I stood feet from it, gazing up under my umbrella, the light from the tree illuminating the rain as it continued to be the only sound of the early morning.

When my friends arrived and we made our way over to the photo spot, we took turns taking each other's picture. It was a pretty impressive setup. Even *I* couldn't believe we were getting such amazing and unlimited access, and I was the one who'd planned it. We stood in front of the lighted angel statues, the ones holding their trumpets, and there was this perfect spot where the angels were on either side of you and the tree behind you. There we were, in the dark of early morning, the only ones around.

We were also getting soaked, and it was raining so hard that I wasn't willing to lower my umbrella when it was my turn. You could say it ruins the photo, but the thing is, I think it actually *makes* the photo. Because without it, how would I remember that morning's weather? Without the umbrella and the look on my face that says both *"I'm so glad I'm doing this"* and *"I sincerely wish I were not doing this,"* how would I have as accurately captured the moment?

The group of us settled into a nearby diner for some breakfast—still dark outside, still dripping water—and by the time we'd finished eating and left, the Today crew was filming just outside. Tourists who'd come to watch were huddled in the background, crowding under umbrellas, trying to protect handwritten signs that couldn't survive the onslaught. A couple from our group opted to stay and join— we were, after all, already wet—but I peeled off. There would be other mornings for Today. Because I *lived* here.

It was almost light as I walked home, and despite the chilling wetness that enveloped every part of me, I couldn't help feeling like I'd gotten away with something. I'd gotten something most people wouldn't get, didn't even know *how* to get. I think what the feeling boiled down to was that I'd gotten exactly what I wanted. Merry Christmas to me.

Sidebar: The Space Paradox and How I Threw My Back Out at Coney Island

New York City can play tricks on you, mostly when it comes to space. Because, truly, there isn't any. You live in a studio apartment. The streets are always crowded. Some days you can't even get far enough away from other people to not be constantly smelling someone's cologne, their hair product, their body odor. It even comes through the vents in your apartment. Other people's cigarette smoke, their bacon frying.

This all came to a head the night I went to Madison Square Garden. It's such an iconic venue, one that had been on my list ever since moving to town. So I went to see the Cavs play the Knicks, unsure as to what exactly it was that I was seeing. Because Manhattan isn't like other cities, with space to build large, rectangular venues that sit completely above ground and take up healthy chunks of real estate. No, Manhattan's iteration of The Venue is partially underground. It's got multiple levels of seating, each of which cascades down over the level below it, such that a portion of my view that night was the level of seating just above me. The seats extended forward and down in a way I'm not entirely sure how it was supported.

The seating was so distracting that it made it difficult to focus on the game or to even *see* it. There was really only a small window through which I could view the court, and while the entire court was visible, nothing else was. No looking up into the vastness of the crowds. No looking up at a jumbotron or looking around in awe at the sheer number of New Yorkers out supporting their team.

I'd never seen an event through this kind of lens or felt so limited while in a structure of this size. It was a kind of claustrophobia I hadn't felt since having a series of MRIs when I was twenty years old. Then, of course, I'd literally been trapped in a small cell, unable to so much as roll over or raise my arm. Madison Square Garden was not so paralyzing; I could, after all, stand up and cheer or go to the concession stand and buy nachos. But I was constantly aware of how little space I had. It's as if all that existed was this little section of fans who had nowhere to go, because we could not see beyond our limited line of sight. To be honest, the whole thing made me feel slightly ill.

On the other hand, New York City is enormous and takes up so much space that one can travel for an hour by train and *still be in it*. Coney Island is one such example. It's literally the last stop on the D line, a train I switched to from the 6 line and then rode for close to an hour before arriving at Brooklyn's southernmost tip.

I'd always wanted to visit Coney Island, if for no other reason than it's mentioned on virtually every New York-based sitcom. There's always a Coney Island episode.

Someone goes. Someone tries to go. Someone ends up naked on the subway while trying to go. I pictured a place not unlike Disneyland in its overabundance of theme and nostalgia and unhealthy food options. Disneyland may have been a bit farfetched, but I wouldn't say my expectations were entirely wrong.

The biggest problem with Coney Island was trying to balance my intake of copious amounts of junk food with my level of uncertainty as to how much the rides, all new to me, were going to mess me up. Vomit is always the worst possible outcome; feeling like I'm going to vomit being only slightly better. And while I stay away from any ride that would very obviously be more than I can handle, there are always a few gambles.

The biggest question for me was the Cyclone, the large, old coaster that Coney Island is widely known for. I knew it would probably push my limits, but the friends I'd come with were going, and as we stood in line after buying $10 tickets, I watched car after car careen down the hills, trying to determine just how intense it got. It looked like something I could handle. Which I did, with no hint of vomiting, the only negative side effect being the roughness of such an old track which left my back thoroughly jostled. It took me a couple of weeks to recover.

There were other interesting rides—the classic swings and the strange horse-themed ride that you went on while lying down, on your stomach, facing forward. If anything was going to make me puke, it would have been that one. Especially after eating cheese fries at Nathan's. But rides don't have much to do with the point I'm trying to make, which is that after having traveled all that distance, here you were, still in New York City. Here you were, at the ocean, at a theme park, walking down the boardwalk. Here you were, feeling as light and unencumbered as you'd felt since moving in. It's not as if there weren't other people around. There were lots. But there was open space, water, boats, sun.

In the picture of me walking on the boardwalk for the first time, it's almost like the crowds parted, like I'm the only one, even though I can see families walking toward the beach, couples waiting in line for food. It's one of my favorite pictures taken of me in New York, and I looked at it whenever I needed reminding that there was more to this place than subways and street lights.

The trip to Coney Island wasn't a cure to the claustrophobia that descended from time to time on the island. It was simply a reprieve. Much like a building rooftop, like the stellar one my friend's Mom had and once invited us to for an evening meal. The sun was making its way down, and I couldn't pull myself away from the roof's edge. Overlooking a busy midtown street, the lights from buildings and cars just starting to stand out against the changing sky, I was suddenly above it, away from it. Noises drifted up slowly, and even though I was in the thick of it, I was also, somehow, out of it. Completely. It was like floating above your own reality. Wearing a bright red jacket and a pixie cut, it's another picture someone snapped, me looking down at the streets below, that became precious in its reminder that perhaps there was enough space in this city for us all.

GOING

KNOWING MY LEASE WOULD SOON BE UP, AND knowing equally well that I couldn't stay put with the bitch of a cat-hating woman below me, I began to search for a new apartment. I turned to Craigslist, as I had before I moved to Cleveland, and then again before I moved to New York.

Ideally I would have preferred to find another apartment on the Upper East Side. I was used to the area, settled, and I felt safe and structured there. Plus, it would make for an easier move. Not that I really had any idea how I would move *anywhere*. A friend of mine had recently done it, and she'd lugged her belongings tote by tote through the city streets on foot. I'd felt sorry for her, this waif of a girl, pausing on the stairwell of my building to catch her breath as she schlepped a few totes up to my apartment. I'd offered to store them for her before her new apartment was ready, and as I raced down the stairs to relieve her and carry the totes the rest of the way up, I was shocked by how heavy they were. I couldn't believe she'd walked so far with them. It must have taken her hours. And this was just one load. It's enough to make a girl never want to move, ever.

And so I began searching for apartments within my neighborhood, realizing pretty quickly that the trouble with this plan was that staying on the Upper East Side would not let me reach one of my main goals for moving. Removing myself from my downstairs neighbor was Priority One, but second only to that was the compelling need I felt to pay less in rent.

I wasn't working at this point, and while I had plenty of money in the bank, when you're not sure exactly how long your funds will need to stretch, it seems downright irresponsible to be unemployed and paying almost $2,500 per month in rent. Yet I couldn't find anything in my general area of town that was much, if any, less costly. If I wanted to knock, say, $1,000 off my rent and still live alone, I'd have to venture off into uncharted waters.

I'd have to dig deep into my reserve of pride and bravery.

I'd have to do what many a friend before me had done out of simple necessity.

I'd have to move to Harlem.

The first apartment I looked at was off of Park Avenue. Now, forty blocks *lower*, living off of Park Avenue would be a different story. A luxurious story. But the Harlem side of Park Avenue is nothing to write home about, unless it's to tell your mother that you're a little afraid for your life. The apartment off of Park was incredibly tiny. Perhaps not much different than the darling little writer's studio I'd been living in, but the layout of this new place was so haphazard—kitchen in the back, a couple of steps leading to the living room, even more steps leading to where the bed was elevated on a platform of sorts by the window—that it gave the whole thing a crowded, cluttered feel.

The biggest problem I saw was the potential for noise. The apartment was right next to the train tracks, and being on the ground floor, the window that the bed was up against was positioned right along the sidewalk. Noisy, but also incredibly vulnerable. From a safety standpoint, I knew that's how I'd feel sleeping so close to strangers walking home from the train. It reminded me of the place my worthless real estate broker had scrambled to show me when I'd first been in town to find an apartment. Part underwhelming, part disturbing, and part clarity over not at all being able to picture yourself calling it home.

My second attempt at finding a Harlem apartment was located north and west of the one on Park. It was not near a train, and what sold me before I'd even seen the inside were the pictures posted on the ad. I'm not sure what it is, but there are certain spaces in this world that will strike each of us as the perfect kind of charming. And this apartment, also a studio, had been decorated so expertly—lace and beads and fabric falling from the loft bed to create a curtain that hid the makeshift closet—that I simply had to see it.

Meeting the landlord did not go as planned—some mix-up on his part regarding the time and some other activity that prevented him from either notifying me or answering his phone—but eventually I did see the apartment and learn that its current occupants were expecting a baby and relocating to Brooklyn in order to have more space. I met them—a lovely, professional couple from South America who oozed about the apartment and how much they loved both the building and the neighborhood—a couple of times before moving in, and soon realized that much of what had made the apartment so special in its charm and character and decoration was them, their style and energy.

The landlord had started off the appointment by mentioning all the other people who were looking at the apartment, and I didn't have any reason not to believe him. An odd man, older, fat, and incredibly scatterbrained, his wife handled all the paperwork and tenant monies, even though I never met her in person. I only ever saw her from a distance. She was young, beautiful, easily thirty years his junior, and from some Spanish-speaking country. They, along with her mother, lived in the building next door to the one at which I was looking, and I couldn't help but wonder how the arrangement came to be. I suppose there are certain sets of circumstances that would make the idea of moving to America to live with an ugly, old, fat property manager seem appealing, and it is perhaps the great success of my life that I have never known those circumstances.

By the end of that first appointment, the landlord had stopped playing hard to get and offered me the apartment. I've never been sure if it's because he'd been lying about the other people he'd been showing it to or if he simply decided I was the one he liked best, but he pronounced me, rather effusively, to be an incredibly nice, sweet, and sincere person, exactly the kind he wanted living in his building.

And so I cut a check for first and last month's rent and returned to the Upper East Side with a copy of the freshly-signed contract and a bag of celebratory macaroons from the local bakery. I was as excited to be getting away from my downstairs neighbor as I was to be saving almost $1,000 each month in rent. I was also excited that, much like my first Manhattan apartment, I'd found it on only my second try. But mostly I was excited to have found another little corner of the city that I could call my own.

I'd noticed on the back of the door to my soon-to-be apartment that the South American couple had adhered a laminated map of Harlem, complete with a few of their favorite places and things marked in ballpoint pen. In the center of 119th Street between Adam Clayton Powell and Frederick Douglass was a building circled and marked, "Home." It struck me in that instant, not just that it was about to be *my* home, or that it had been theirs, but that this was home for *so many* people, millions, this cacophonous mix of subways and stairwells, of bellmen and Broadway. So different than what most of us call home, and yet what defines home has nothing to do with square footage, or with how many floors you have to walk up just to get to the front door. Home is simply the place you keep coming back to. Home is where you already are, at this moment, because you've marked it in such a way that you can never be lost from it.

COMING

IT ALL CAME TO A HEAD WITH THE WOMAN
downstairs one night while I was making dinner. I hadn't
noticed my cat doing anything in particular, but then again,
she was *never* doing anything in particular, other than
moving. Yet amidst the pasta water beginning to boil on the
stove, I heard the familiar sound of discontent being yelled
up at me from below. Only this time, I thought I heard
something else. A door slam.

Before I knew it, this old, somewhat frail night shopper
had climbed the flight of stairs between our apartments and
was pounding on my door.

What on earth?

It's the first time she'd ever confronted me, and I had to
think fast. I figured seeing the cat would only make her mad,

but at the same time, I wanted her to see this tiny creature for which she blamed all her discontent. I wanted her to see the five pounds of stripes and fur that appear practically dwarfed when in the arms of an adult human. I wanted her to feel just as small and dwarfed.

And so I scooped up my cat and opened the door.

I don't think she expected to see the cat, thrust right in between us and impossible to ignore, and she paused for a moment before speaking in a tone she was working hard to pass off as controlled and reasonable.

"Hi there," she began. "I'm downstairs and I'm really bothered by the noise that cat is making up here."

"*This* cat?" I played along. I was not in the mood to be bullied.

"Yes, it sounds like a jungle tiger cat galloping across my ceiling."

"She weighs five pounds."

"Well, it's really hard with my treatments and there must be something you can do about it."

"I'm not sure what your treatments have to do with it. I'm sorry it bothers you, but there's nothing else I can do."

"How can you say there's nothing else you can do?"

"Because we've already put in additional rugs, followed by carpet. Short of locking the cat in the bathroom, what would you suggest I do?"

"You can get the fuck out."

"Excuse me?"

"Get. The fuck. Out."

This one hit me like a sucker punch and knocked all my courage and resolve aside. How dare she. How dare she reduce me to feeling so belittled and unwanted. How dare she use the F-word to my fucking face.

By this time my landlord had heard the commotion and had come out into the hall.

"What are you *doing?*" she asked my downstairs neighbor, approaching my door.

"I was just bringing up ideas for what could be done about the cat," the woman said.

"Telling me to get the fuck out? *That's* your idea?" I shot back.

I let my landlord take over the conversation, their words disappearing in the hallway as I walked the few steps back over to my now boiling pasta and began to mindlessly stir. I felt in this moment as low as I had ever felt since moving to New York. It had beaten me. This woman had beaten me. I began to cry, a kind of helpless, unstoppable cry one only experiences when she feels completely defeated.

When the downstairs neighbor returned to her apartment, my landlord stepped inside my still-open door and apologized profusely, even though I'd heard it all before. The woman downstairs was rotten. Everyone felt for me. They were all here for me. Except that it had been me, not any of them, across the doorway when this bitch of a woman looked me in the eye and told me to get the fuck out of this building. It had been me each time my floor rap-rap-rapped from the handle of a broom. It had been me each time something got yelled up from her apartment. It had always been just me. Not any of them.

Seeing my tears, my landlord enveloped me in a hug, which made me cry harder. Of course there was the awkwardness of breaking down in front of this woman with whom I didn't have a particularly close relationship—a woman who had come out of her apartment to rescue me while wearing a rather threadbare robe that only came down to her mid-thigh. There was also the joint sorrow we both felt over a battle we couldn't win or even remotely fix. But mostly there was the looming realization that I couldn't stay. That living in this darling apartment was bringing me down in a way I could no longer make up for with all the things I loved about it.

When my lease was up, I took my cat and put forty blocks between us and the woman downstairs.

Sidebar: Penn Station and an Obligatory Mention of the Naked Cowboy

In pretty short order, I developed a crush on Penn Station. What I felt for Penn Station *before* this crush was fear and intimidation. But then again, that's how I initially felt about almost all means of transportation in New York.

While living on the far East Side, my nearest subway option, which wasn't even very near, was the 6 train, which I'd have to take to a transfer point, maybe Grand Central or Union Square, in order to get to many of my final destinations. It's easy to become comfortable with the subway though, thanks largely to the maps that show how everything connects and the way that apps such as Stop Hop could take those maps and spit out a number of different routes based on your starting and ending locations. The subway is also the cheapest option, a $2.50 swipe getting you basically as far as you need to go within any of the city's boroughs.

It's amusing to me that taxis are so prevalent in movies and shows set in New York. Not because there aren't a shit ton of them around, but because the average New Yorker, which is most of them, doesn't use cabs to get around.

The only times I ever did were to and from the airport when I was traveling for work because I knew the company would reimburse me. But on my own dime? Not a chance.

That did leave the question then of how to get to the airport when I *wasn't* taking a taxi. Even after finding out from my friend Molly that I could simply walk a few blocks and be picked up by a bus that would take me all the way to LaGuardia for just a couple of bucks, it took me a while to come around to the idea. A bus? Really? She'd actually proposed buses as a good transportation option for me as soon as I'd moved to the East Side. There were bus stops all over, apparently, but I'd resisted. It just seemed like a lot to keep track of. A whole new schedule and system to learn.

Of course, like so many ideas that seem annoying to me at first,* once I tried it—both to the airport and to simply get from East Side to West Side and back again—I was completely converted. I couldn't believe I'd been missing out, and if there's one thing that changed my life for the better while living on the Upper East Side of Manhattan, it's the bus.

A single swipe of your metro card could still get you almost anywhere the bus would take you, and what sold me right away was how much better it is to be above ground than below. Below ground you never really know quite where you are, just somewhere between two stops. And if there's a problem, instead of being crammed against a smattering of strangers and trapped until the situation is resolved, you're sitting in a cushioned seat and able to simply get off the bus.

Most importantly, you can see where you're going,

---

*Like iPods, iPhones, smart TVs, and any of the Marvel superhero movies.

what you're passing on the way to your destination. I have such clear memories of driving through the city on fall and winter nights, when it got dark early, and feeling such pure contentment as we passed the shops and apartments all lit up inside. I'd be bundled in my seat, hat and scarf and gloves and coat, watching the scenery become more familiar as we wound our way closer to my 1st Avenue stop. Stepping off, I'd walk the short distance to my apartment, music playing on my headphones, filled with a sense of pride for having gotten the hang of it, this bus thing. I was a New Yorker coming home after a long day. I was a user of public transportation. Being raised in a very small town, it's something that seemed even more amazing to me. That this is how I got around. That this was real life.

Now, adding *trains* into the mix? Enter Penn Station. I might not have used the station as anything other than a subway stop had my brother not been in the Airforce and stationed in New Jersey during the time I lived in Manhattan. In order to visit, I needed to hop a train to the Hamilton station along the New Jersey Transit Line, about a 60-minute ride if you could catch an express, up to 90 minutes if you couldn't.

The first time I did this was the weekend I'd come to Manhattan to look for a place to live. My real estate broker had botched my request, so I'd had to conduct a search on my own, miraculously coming away with a darling studio apartment. I was on the train to New Jersey to see my brother, his wife, and their brand new baby when I got word that I'd been offered the apartment. Reading a book, the late afternoon sun sinking in the sky, I felt such overwhelming relief, both for finding the apartment and for successfully getting myself on the correct train. The train part of Penn Station operates on a number of tracks spread out over a considerable distance. After purchasing a ticket either from a kiosk or from a teller after waiting in line, you head over to one of the display monitors to find out what track you'll be on. The tricky part here is that they don't post the track numbers until about two minutes before the train arrives. So you have to be watching. And as soon as the number posts, you hurry down to the appropriate track and hope you make it in time. It's funny really, especially if it's not you having to hurry, this mass lobby exodus as large groups scatter with each new track posting.

I made this New Jersey voyage about once a month, always for a weekend, and always with an empty suitcase to fill with groceries that were regularly priced. Those weekends were such a reprieve for me. Away from the chaos of the city, away from the downstairs neighbor who yelled and swore each time my cat ran around. She surely yelled and swore while I was gone, but at least I wasn't there to hear it, which is why a sad sort of stress descended on me each time I was on the train headed back to Penn Station.

Penn Station brought me my parents, when they came to New Jersey to see the baby and then took the train in to spend a day with me in the city. It was their first time in New York, and despite some minor self-consciousness on my part—showing them my tiny apartment, I wondered if they were at all concerned for their adult daughter and her cupboard of instant food products and preoccupation with not upsetting the woman downstairs—it was one of those unbelievable moments you could never have predicted. Me and my small-town parents in Times Square, Mom inadvertently snapping a picture of the Naked Cowboy. As a joke, my brother programmed the picture as what would come up on the screen any time she called my dad. It makes me laugh to this day.

I think what Penn Station became to me then was a conduit of sorts. One that, on my own and far from home, could temporarily connect me to my family, or at least a piece of it. It wasn't just those trips to New Jersey. It was also the times my brother and his wife came to see me, arriving at Penn Station with big smiles and warm hugs. We went for cookies in the West Village. We went to Tiffany's to ogle at the jewelry. We met up at Columbus Circle, me strapping my baby nephew into a carrying band, his little body facing mine as we walked, while my sister-in-law ran an errand.

That one was my favorite, just me and my nephew on our own in the city. I walked us over to Central Park, his curious eyes taking everything in as I did my best to show him all the best parts. I loved introducing him to a place I considered so iconic. A place he'd likely return to one day when he was grown. Maybe he'd feel the sensation of having been there before. Maybe he'd feel nothing.

I certainly felt something that day, walking back to Columbus Circle with the weight of this little person strapped to my middle. By the time we returned, he was sound asleep, and I couldn't have felt more love for anyone. Penn Station had brought me that.

GOING

THE MACY'S THANKSGIVING DAY PARADE HAD
never been a part of my childhood. I have almost no memory
of ever watching it, partly because it just wasn't one the things
that we did. Watching a bunch of floats roll by didn't scream
"gratitude," and we filled the day with other things. Well,
basically eating. Because we can all be grateful for food.

The other reason I had almost no exposure to the parade
as a youngster was that we went through long stretches without
cable television. It wasn't any kind of financial issue, in that
they weren't cutting off our service because we weren't paying
our bill. My parents would simply, from time to time, decide
to have it turned off. They didn't want us watching a ton of
TV, most shows being deemed inappropriate anyway, so often
they opted to do without. They'd bring it back for things like
the Olympics, the NBA playoffs if Portland had made it, and

once we discovered The X-Files, but TV played a very minor role in our lives as a family. For this I feel very fortunate.

Truthfully, I never felt like I was missing out on the parade or that my holiday was somehow less complete or authentic. From the glimpses I'd seen—all balloons and marching bands and B-list celebrities lip-synching to their hit songs—it was the same thing every year. And that thing wasn't particularly exciting. I'd rather watch the dog show that came on after the parade, which, surprisingly, is something that *did* become Thanksgiving tradition in our home for a number of years. Complete with guesses and scorecards and a winner. Now *that* was excitement. Especially the year that the Scottish Deerhound, our family's favorite breed, made it into the Best in Show competition.*

Despite not having any attachment to the Macy's parade, once I moved to New York, it suddenly felt like something I ought to experience. I'd moved in early October, so by the end of November, I'd gained some confidence in my surroundings. I knew where to go, I knew how things worked, mostly, and I wanted to make the most out of my time in this incredible city. So when my friend Molly mentioned that she and a group of her friends went to the parade every year and watched it live, I decided to tag along.

Central Park can be unnerving in the dark, especially

---

*Scottish Deerhounds are so beloved to me that a few years ago while visiting Scotland for the first time, I kept hoping I'd see one in its native land. Surely the countryside ran plush with them. Surely people had them as pets. I finally asked the guide giving me a tour of the Highlands if there were a lot of them here. He replied that there weren't. That they were just big expensive pets and no one had them anymore. I saw some of the most beautiful slices of earth I'd ever seen on that trip, yet still left those green hillsides a bit let down that I hadn't seen a single Scottish Deerhound.

when there's not another soul in sight. And so I walked quickly that Thanksgiving, at 4:00 in the morning, from my apartment on the far East Side to the parade route along Central Park West. It was not warm, and I was already cold in my long johns and coat, hat, gloves, and scarf. Molly's friends had arrived even earlier and snagged us a spot right in the front. We were near one of the blocks in the high seventies, Central Park across the street, and the parade wouldn't be coming through for another six hours.

Six hours.

We kept busy as best we could, chatting and playing games, even though it seemed too cold for either activity and the expanding crowd soon pressured us into standing instead of sitting on the blanket we'd spread out over our little block of sidewalk. I felt a little bit bad pretending to be one of them; my only connection to the group was Molly and I'd still been snug in my bed when the first of them had shown up to claim such a prime spot. I'm not kidding when I say we were in the very front. No one to try to see over or between once the parade started because we were it. We were the front.

I wandered over to Starbucks a couple of times during those hours for hot chocolate. It didn't do as much as I'd hoped to keep me warm, but the long lines provided a distraction, and the bathroom provided relief from all the hot chocolate I was drinking. Mostly I kept looking up at the buildings just above us, the apartments that lined Central Park West. These people had only to look out their windows and they'd have a perfect view of the parade. And how was this *possible*? Who *were* these people who owned these apartments, who could afford them, who lived in them, or knew people who lived in them and could secure an invitation?

Who were these people that could wait until 10:00 a.m. to crawl out of bed and still have the best view in the entire city? And all while wearing their pajamas. Were they as happy as I imagined them to be, holding children up to windows and pointing, everyone smiling while the smell of turkey and stuffing wafted in from expensively-furnished custom kitchens? Even after the parade started and I became transfixed by my own proximity to it, my eyes kept wandering up to these people, to watch them watching the same thing I was, yet experiencing something entirely different.

The parade did not disappoint, and in the pictures Molly took of me, there's nothing between me and the balloons. Nothing between me and the parade itself. Just me and Snoopy. And isn't that just a little bit incredible? This thing streaming through the homes of millions of Americans. Not *my* home, of course, but everyone else's. This thing that happens in this place every year now intersecting with me because I am now in this place.

My friends who saw the pictures commented on how cool it was, on how they'd wondered if I would be there, on how they were so glad I'd done it. Because who *has*? Aside from the people living in those Central Park West apartments, how many of us can say we've had a front row seat to such a widespread holiday festivity?

I'd been told that the parade ends with a literal explosion of confetti that gets shot into the streets and sidewalks, such that you find it everywhere, for months to come. And this may have been my favorite part. The colorful shower of paper that had me reaching out to catch it, to grab it, to fill my pockets with it, to preserve something for a later date, when I needed reminding. Even the way the street looked once the confetti had blown through. It was the best part of the whole day.

Walking home on legs so cold I could not feel them, the park felt alive and welcoming. I was exhausted and chilled to the bone, but my pockets were full of what would come to be one of the best things I collected from my time in New York. I would never have an apartment along Central Park West, but I was immeasurably blessed, and when I returned to my little studio, I would turn on the dog show and find out if the Scottish Deerhound had made it through.

COMING

MOST OF THE TIME IN NEW YORK, I FELT BRAVE
and pretty kick-ass for being there. For doing what I was
doing. For quitting my job and chasing my dream and going
all in when it came to the pursuit of a new career path.

Most of the time.

Or at least some of the time.

Occasionally.

What I felt when I wasn't feeling kick-ass was rather
panicked about what the hell I had done. You first have to
understand that doing this—moving to New York City and
quitting my job—wasn't a decision I had made lightly. Nor
was it one I made right away, or without a lot of worry over
its effects. Working with a life coach on how to go about
making this change, the whole process took some time. Not

only to map out the steps and actions I needed to take, but also to even come to the decision in the first place. To *do* it. Most of my hesitation was financial, in that only an idiot quits a job she doesn't hate that pays a very high salary in a city with an exceptionally low cost of living. So yes, I worried about the change that would come to my lifestyle, namely, the need to budget. But more than that, the financial piece that gave me the most heartburn was not how this would affect me, but how it might potentially affect others, or my ability to help others. I thought of my parents and other family members. What if the time came when they needed financial help or support? What if I was forever giving up my ability to do that? As a financially stable adult, I felt some responsibility to my family members to stay that way.

But you can't base your life decisions on other people, nor can you operate under the assumption that it's all up to you. You can't put that much pressure on yourself when it comes to the lives and well beings of other people. And so I pulled the trigger, even though the excitement and satisfaction I felt came with an equal if not greater amount of anxiety.

Most of my worry once I was an unemployed Manhattanite came down to these two things: 1) Would my savings last as long as it took to finish my gemology program and find a job in the industry? And 2) Would I even be able to *find* a job in the industry? Or, more to the point, would this even work?

In case this is in any way unclear to you, these are pretty big concerns. The kind that loom every time you write your rent check, buy a plane ticket home, go see a Broadway play, or even pick up your weekly groceries. *How long will this money need to last? How long until I have a gemology job?*

They are the kinds of concerns that can cloud the lens of everyday life with a film of exaggerated crappiness. A man on the subway thinks I'm a lesbian because of my pixie cut, and the stereotypical observation reduces me to pieces because *I am freaking unemployed.* A homeless person chides me for only giving him a one dollar bill and I feel a fiery shame because *I have no money coming in.* The woman downstairs yells obscenities up at me when my cat runs around and I am overcome by self-doubt because *I used to have a two-story home and health insurance.*

While on a trip visiting family, this all came to a head in a way I wouldn't have predicted but that didn't surprise me. During what started out as a simple conversation about my new life in New York, I ended up in tears over what felt a lot like a plight. Because what had I done? What if it was a mistake? What if I could no longer afford to come visit them, to see my nephews as they grew up? What if I couldn't find a job even with a gemology diploma or never again had the financial stability I did while working for Pressure-Sensitive Leader, maxing out my 401K match and enjoying employer-paid insurance premiums? What if that was all gone forever?

Unprepared for such blubbering, my family did a good job of comforting and reassuring, reminding me that there was a long, long way to go before anything about my current status and finances became truly worrisome. Someone even mentioned that for many, my situation was actually enviable. Because how many people would love to quit their steady, uninteresting jobs and pursue a true passion? How many people will never be able to afford such a risk, either because they cannot produce the necessary funds or because they must use those funds to support a spouse and children? How many people are truly so free?

Free.

Is that what I was? Is that what my lens of anxiety was blocking from coming into focus? Is that how I would feel if I could calm the hell down about everything and just enjoy the pursuit of this dream?

I'd like to say I returned from that trip forever changed, no longer encumbered by worries of bills and bank accounts; that none of it phased me anymore. That's not really how it happened, but I do think this conversation did, if nothing else, remind me that even with my worries, with the uncertainties and risk I had invited into my life with these decisions, I was still pretty lucky. Lucky to be focusing all of my efforts on the pursuit of a dream. Because what if I got it? What if my savings sustained me and a new job got me exactly where I wanted to be? The fact is, when you play it safe, when you stay in the steady, uninteresting job, you don't even have that chance.

SIDEBAR: NEW YORK PUBLIC LIBRARY AND HOW MY TEENAGE SELF EVALUATED BOOKS

I blame Manhattan for getting me stuck on the public library system. Not that the concept was a new one. I'd certainly been exposed to libraries while growing up in Oregon, borrowing books from our piddly public branch as well as those even *more* piddly ones at the elementary, junior high, and high schools.

I can still remember the rating system I used upon finishing each book, the titles recorded on lined notebook paper in my uneven handwriting. Using a highly sophisticated series of plus and minus signs, the only criteria I measured was how much the book stirred my newly-developing hormones. If there was lots that set the deepest part of my gut aflutter as I read, then it got a plus sign, or on

rare occasions, *two* plus signs. Why this didn't escalate into an unhealthy attachment to erotica would be an excellent question, except for the fact that I'd had no idea it even existed. Plus, you're only an early teen for so long, and there's a very limited window in which the sensation of butterflies is novel.

As an adult I'd gotten away from the practice of checking out books, mainly because landing a posh corporate job in my mid-twenties in Cleveland meant I had a large salary and a small cost of living. I got in the habit of buying books because I had both the income and the space, so anything I saw that I wanted to read, I just went ahead and bought. And the shelves of books lining my Cleveland house, all held up by kitschy sets of bookends I'd picked out over the years, made me incredibly happy. That is, until I signed the lease on my tiny Manhattan studio and realized I couldn't take them with me.

The lack of space in my New York apartment is what prompted my return to the public library, knowing I no longer had the luxury of buying and collecting books. And I confess that there's a rather magical quality to having a library card for the New York Public Library system. It's part Ghostbusters, I suppose, but mostly it's the comprehension of the vastness that is the public library system in New York. It's realizing you're a part of something so grand, so official, so established. I mean, just *try* and walk past those stone lions at 42nd and Fifth without getting goosebumps. I bet you can't do it.

Not that the lions at 42nd and Fifth is ever where I went to check out books, my own local branch on 79th Street being so much more convenient, but that's another thing that's so great about libraries in New York. There are so many of them. And to know that I could request a particular book, *any* book, and it'd be ready for me to pick up at the 79th Street branch in a matter of days made me feel like I had the whole world in my hands. Because didn't I?

Any book.

And once being notified that my request was ready for pickup, there was something equally magical about striding directly to the Hold shelves, finding my name, and pulling the specific book away from its neighbors with my index finger. There's a certain sort of confidence in a girl who is going to the library to pick up a book, who places it on the counter with the kind of contented firmness that says, *"This is the one I wanted."*

I took a picture of myself walking home from the library the day I got my New York library card. It'd been a long time since I'd even *had* a library card, as the only times I'd gone to the library in Cleveland were to admire the building—a Harry Potteresque mansion full of interesting rooms and storybook towers that had been donated by a wealthy family—or to buy books from their biannual book sales.

So something about owning a library card—about being a part of this vast literary network of pages and chapters and volumes—felt worth capturing, which is why I broke the unspoken No Selfies on the Street clause of NYC Code and snapped an image of myself, smiling, wearing headphones, the library card held up with pride. I'd just gotten a pixie cut, and there's so much New York in me in that instant that I somehow managed to look simultaneously familiar and unrecognizable. My mom later told me it was perhaps her favorite picture of me. Like, ever. I'll chalk it up to the value of reading, and to the happiness I felt at having unlimited access while living in the city. (I could also chalk it up to the pixie, which was pretty badass.)

Reading is something I was able to do a lot of while living in New York, and in some rather interesting places. The gardens at St. Luke's church, underneath the Brooklyn Bridge, museum lobbies, delayed subway cars, Washington Square Park with a lapful of Amy's bread and Murray's cheese, cross-town buses, cronut lines, restaurant tables, building rooftops, cathedral pews, and the sun-strewn steps of my apartment building. My favorite, of course, was Central Park.

Up on the Harlem end where there are far fewer bodies, there were some trees I'd settle under during the spring months before it got too hot. Lying directly on the grass, tummy down, knees bent back and bare feet crossed behind me, I'd notice the blotchy pattern of shade and sun hitting each page, sometimes needing to hold them down so the wind didn't turn them before I was ready. The whole setup felt like perfection. Because I'm pretty sure it was. And my ticket to all of it was the library card that said I was in the club. It gave me the swagger to pick up books and snap street selfies and while away afternoons in no one's company but my current protagonist.

Coming

AS I GOT CLOSER AND CLOSER TO COMPLETING all the coursework required prior to attempting my big final gemology test, the one that required 100 percent accuracy in order to pass, there was still something that eluded me: I'd never been able to actually *get* a 100 percent on any of the practice assignments.

By this point in my final course, all my assignments were basically mock tests, where I'd get a box of completely random stones and have to identify them. And I always got something wrong. Usually just one or two, but still, if perfection is the requirement, it seemed like I wasn't yet where I needed to be.

And so I spent additional time in the student laboratory on campus, practicing on other stones. I recognized a few areas that were tricky for me and spent some time working on only those. I looked at boxes of sapphires to get better at identifying natural from synthetic. I looked at wheels of garnets, all different colors, to get the hang of separating almandine from andradite from pyrope, whose refractive indices and hues weren't all that different. I looked at chalcedony, a tricky family of opaque, patterned varieties that were difficult to identify. Example: Jasper doesn't have to be but is typically red. Sard is described as reddish-brown. Carnelian as brownish-red. Clear as mud?

And then there was color, because one of the hardest things for me to get a handle on was the fine line between one color and the one right next to it on the color wheel. Gems are all labeled in ways that leave room for two identifying colors, so you can have bluish green, but you can also have greenish blue. And what makes a stone orangey red as opposed to reddish orange?

You could say it's simply that the color listed last is most dominant, but is it really that easy? Ruby, after all, is the same material as sapphire, simply with the presence of chromium which colors it red. The core body color of red makes it a ruby, but de-saturate that red just enough, and what you have is a pink sapphire. Ruby and pink sapphire became my nemeses, in that I'd always study and study one of them, label it as one or the other, and inevitably be wrong. Not the rich, full-bodied rubies, of course, but the ones with less red in them. At some point, they were no longer rubies. But what exactly was that point? How pink was *pink*?

Every morning I left my Harlem apartment and walked

down to 110th Street to catch the subway to Times Square, then worked my way through the crowded few blocks to get to campus in the diamond district on 47th Street. It wasn't a commute, yet that's what it felt like to me. It was satisfying in that way. Even though I was wearing jeans and sneakers instead of a pressed suit and heels and no one would pay me for the day's work. Even though this was a short-term gig that would soon be over. I embraced every purposeful trip downtown. *This* was what I was doing. *This* was my perfect and fleeting reality.

And I did get better. As I practiced in the lab, I was concurrently finishing up my final course assignments. When I turned in my very last assignment, I hoped I would finally achieve that elusive 100 percent. That perfect score. Yet when my instructor returned the now-graded worksheet, I felt certain there must be some mistake. I'd missed seven. *Seven.* More than I had ever missed on any assignment. Even the early ones when I knew almost nothing about what I was doing. *Seven.* Surely this was someone else's paper.

To understand the rather desperate sense of depression and doom that settled over me after such a blow—remember, the next step would have been to take the big final test, the one requiring a perfect score, a score I had never gotten—you have to understand a little more about the nature of what it was I was trying to accomplish. I'd quit my job to make this happen. I wanted to be a gemologist. Now. Not someday. Not maybe in a few years. *Now.* So I'd quit my job to study full time. And I'd gotten lucky in that as I neared the completion of my graduate gemology program, I was offered and accepted an amazing job at the world's largest gem institute. Which meant my flexible schedule for studying and test-taking was quickly coming to a close.

When I looked at the calendar and compared the time I had left before starting my new job with the schedules of the campus lab and testing centers, which were not open every day, there were, in fact, only two weeks left that I had to work with. I figured I'd need one of these weeks to prac-tice—I'd missed *seven*—and the other week to take the big final test, which took all day and which most people had to take an average of six times before getting the necessary perfect score. If I didn't pass on any of my attempts, I'd have to pack up and move across the country and start my job and wait until I had vacation time before resuming my test attempts. Only by then I'd be much less practiced. I'd have forgotten some of what I'd worked so hard to grasp in the lab. I'd be even less likely to get a perfect score. Yes, *this was the time*. The *only* time. This was the time to do the thing I had come here to do. But *seven*? How could I possibly rally to perfection?

That night I cried on the subway. And instead of going home after exiting the 110th Street station, I walked the few hundred yards to my friend Molly's apartment. I was sobbing by the time she answered the door, and as she enveloped me in a hug, I whimpered my way through an explanation of the seven missed stones and how impossible this was. That if I didn't pass this test, then the whole thing would be for naught. That I had to do this thing that I clearly wasn't ready to do.

Molly told me later that when she opened the door and saw me in hysterics, she assumed one of my family members had died, and for a second I felt silly for being so dramatic. Over gems. But this was the goal of my entire New York existence. How could I leave and still not be a gemologist?

Back in the lab for my final week of practice, I focused on those things that tended to trip me up, going over them again and again. I had my instructor quiz me on color differences. I had him grade worksheet after worksheet, and toward the end of the week, he told me I was ready.

"But I missed seven on my last assignment," I reasoned.

"I've been watching you," he said. "And with your care and methodology, I think you're ready to take the test."

The very idea seemed so absurd. I'd literally never before gotten the score I needed to get. But I, also literally, was out of time. I had one week left. And a holiday week at that. So four potential opportunities to pass my big final test. And so I held my breath and called the registration desk and booked myself a spot for each of the four days.

Because *this* was the time. It had to be.

GOING

THE PIXIE CUT HAD BEEN BREWING.

I think, deep down, every woman wants to try it. She just has to get to the point where she has sufficiently beaten back the societal notion that femininity equals hair.

This is not to say that I walked into the 86th Street Aveda salon with what I would call confidence. It was more like fear. Or at least a sense of loss over the effect this would have on my, yes, femininity.

"Just needing to trim up that bob?" the stylist asked as she draped a black cape across the front of me, clearly expecting something different from the girl with the bangs and shoulder-length hair who'd just hopped up into her adjustable stool seat.

"Actually," I said, "I've been thinking about a pixie."

I saw it flash across her eyes, if only for a moment, that anxious rush of *shitshitshit*. Not something that could simply be trimmed, lightened, and feathered, this was something that could easily be screwed up. Even if not in execution—even if she delivered a flawlessly textbook pixie—the odds of me walking out of the salon somewhere on the spectrum of Displeased or even Freaking Out were now automatically much higher.

But it was only a flash, and then she was back, this curvy, twenty-something Latina with tight jeans and high heels and a mop of stylishly tussled dyed hair. She had just the sort of edge you'd want in someone performing such a major change to your appearance. And while she did ask if I wouldn't rather wait until it wasn't winter so as to keep my neck from being cold, I reasoned I might lose my nerve before spring. Or even before tomorrow.

There's something about long hair on a woman, there really is. It's sexy. And, I'll say it again, feminine. Yet why is it that every time a female celebrity chops all her hair off and the before and after images get plastered on magazine covers and gossip websites, she will inevitably be far more stunning with a pixie? It's as if shedding those layers exposes the real self; the self not hiding behind that femininity, or at least the self that knows that this femininity is strong enough to carry itself without long tresses. A girl who cuts her hair knows something other women do not yet know, and that kind of confidence is as sexy as it is fierce.

Looking at myself in the mirror, newly-shorn, I can't say I rejoiced at finally recognizing my real self. I can't say I even necessarily liked what I saw. It's more that I wondered what the hell I'd just done. And in *winter*, for crying out loud. It just seemed so extreme, and I couldn't undo it.

But this was a time for breaking new ground. So I took a deep breath as the stylist finished me off with a final layer of product. I even followed her to the makeup counter and let her roll on a coat of bright red lipstick.

"I'm telling you," she said, "if you want to wear your hair short you have to step it up in the makeup department. Otherwise you'll look butch."

"Oh, ok. Isn't this a little *too* red?"

"Honey, no. You could not get red enough. In fact, I want you to leave here and walk straight over to Sephora."

And so I walked out into the night, convinced I was a bit of a spectacle.

I have no hair, I have no hair, I have no hair.

People were staring.

I look butch, I look butch, I look butch.

By the time I got to Sephora I had wiped off the lipstick on the back of my hand, but I did go inside and explain my plight. One of the workers promptly gave me a makeover—many layers of heavy eye makeup as well as a re-application of bright red lipstick—and I bought everything she had used on me, already doubting whether I'd ever again want to make myself look like I did in that moment.

I left the store, once again sure everyone was staring, this time at my harlot face, and headed to Times Square where I was meeting a group of girlfriends for dinner and a show.

Despite my total lack of confidence, I was proud of myself for getting the pixie. I snapped several pictures of myself as I walked, trying to get an idea of what it really looked like, and I began to smile as I recognized myself in them. My real self. Perhaps I'd found her after all. Not hiding behind bangs and layers but styled and neatly-coifed, she looked unfettered. She looked aflame. She looked like no one else.

I met up with Molly first, my closest friend in New York. I hadn't told her I was getting the pixie, and I watched her break into a smile from across the street when she saw me.

"There you are," she said, a line we repeated from then on each time one of us got our hair cut.

I loved how this phrase aligned so perfectly with the idea of our real selves.

There's a picture Molly took of me that night—standing across the street from the neon sign of the Brooks Atkinson theater, a taxi cab driving by and my head turned sideways smiling at something down the street—and it just might be the sexiest I've ever looked. Because by then I knew the thing that only women who cut their hair can know.

"Also," Molly said, "I've never seen you wear that much eye makeup."

That's fair.

Sidebar: Broadway and That Time I Said I Didn't Like The Lion King

I first came to New York City as a guest of one of the accounts I managed at a small third-party logistics provider. It was a bit of a big deal at the time, in that no one *else's* accounts were taking them to New York, and the sheer privilege of it all made me a bit drunk with status. My account was *paying* to take me to New York. Flying me out there, putting me up in a hotel, and giving me pocket money to have on hand for food and taxis. Honestly, I felt like a big deal.

Of course, that big deal status deflated as soon as my boss, the CEO of the logistics provider, copied me on the email he sent my account that detailed the requirements of them taking me along. One was that they pay my salary* for the days I was gone, and to my horror, an amount was written into that particular line item. It's not that I hadn't known I was grossly underpaid at the time, it's that my *account* hadn't known, and that information now being public was face-to-palm humiliating, even to a 22-year-old in her first job.

---

*Salary is a generous term here, as I punched a time-card and was paid by the hour.

Being in New York when you're still quite young and have spent your entire life in the West can be hard to process. It's a lot to take in. And when I reflect on this first week I spent there, my memories bring back images of tall buildings grouped together and taxis whizzing by the vendors selling pretzels and street meat. It's hard to get beyond that surface level, especially when you are in town to work and don't really know how to navigate anyway.

But I knew that first time I came to New York that I wanted to see a Broadway show, probably because I come from a family with a deep appreciation for theater and musicals. Not that we were exposed to much culture living in a small timber town 90 minutes away from the nearest performing arts center. But whenever something was there, at the Hult Center in Eugene, my parents made a point of driving us to see it. And I loved it. All of it. I'm sure it's partly because I dreamed that one day I could be a theater performer and live the life that they did. Mostly though, it's because we owned so many soundtracks to musicals, so many video copies of musicals, and I genuinely loved these shows. We were downright *raised* on them.

So almost as soon as I arrived in New York with my work account and had checked into the Roosevelt Hotel, I walked over to Times Square to buy a ticket for the one night off I would have during the week. Of course, when I say *walked over* I mean that I tagged along when another member of our party was headed that way. I'd have had no idea where to go, and even once we got there, it was hard to make sense of all the theaters. I really just wanted a ticket for *anything*, and I tried to take courage as I watched my companion—a twenty-something blonde man who I half hoped would suggest that the two of us go to a show *together*—go in and out of box offices in the fading evening light.

"I'm sorry, they only had one left," he said sheepishly after leaving the Minskoff Theater box office with a single ticket to *The Lion King*.

In the moment I was more disappointed about him not wanting to make a date out of it than I was not getting to see *The Lion King*. As a stage production, it had never much appealed to me. It would be almost a decade later before I finally decided to see it. I'd heard such glorious reviews from friends and family—life-changing, uncontrollable tears— that I could feel myself willing an intense emotional state upon myself as the lights dimmed and the first epic refrain filled the theater. Yet other than the opening number, which is fascinatingly superb, I actually found the whole thing rather slow and boring.*

So, no, it didn't break my heart not to get a ticket to *The Lion King* on my first night in New York. What almost *did* break my heart was the realization that Monday, which would be my night off, was dark. In theater, dark means that there's no show that night, and most theaters take Monday as their dark day.

Determination took over, because there simply *had* to be something playing in this city on a Monday, and when *Phantom of the Opera* turned out to be my only option, I plunked down a chunk of change and walked away with a ticket. Victory if ever there was one.

---

*Yes, I know, I've outed myself as the one person on earth who doesn't like the stage version of *The Lion King*. Boo! Hiss!

It felt ironic, in that I'd spent my adolescence vehemently bashing *Phantom* as having not nearly the amount of feeling and emotion packed into its songs as did *Les Miserables*. And while I still feel that this is an accurate statement, I can tell you that while sitting in the balcony of the Majestic Theater on a Monday night surrounded by jetlagged Chinese tourists who all fell asleep mid-performance, I wept. I wept for the Phantom's predicament, which I'd never before really considered. The whole thing made me desperately sad, in a way I'm not sure I've ever been able to shake. If that is the power of Broadway, then I was on board.

Throughout my time in New York, I saw too many shows to name, to even recall. Broadway, off-Broadway, off-off-Broadway (which, for those keeping track at home, has to do with the number of seats the auditorium has), and it helped that I had a friend who worked in stage management who always had tips on hot shows, or shows I'd never heard of, or discounts to things I wanted to see. As I learned during that first *Phantom of the Opera* performance, theater moves us in ways we may not expect or be prepared for, and when I think of theater in New York, there are a few experiences that stand out.

After an epic breakup several years ago, I ended up with two tickets to *Newsies* and no date. Molly, my stage manager friend and my usual partner in crime when it came to theater in New York, was more than happy to go with me, and bless her heart. I was so lovesick that I spent the whole time we were in line swiveling my neck between various street corners, half convinced my ex would show up in some grand gesture of apology and changed-mindedness.

He didn't.

Funny how it's not always the show but the circumstances surrounding the show that stay with you. While I won't say I felt better after watching those boys sing and dance their way to a news revolution, I can say that I was at least distracted. So distracted that I hadn't noticed as we walked away from the theater what was happening to my hair.

"Tali, stop!" Molly said.

"What?" I asked, thinking she must have seen my ex. He'd come after all!

"Look at your hair!"

My *hair?*

A silly request, in that I couldn't very well see my own hair, but I did notice, both through a sensation now bubbling near my fingertips and from moving my hands somewhat gingerly toward my long hair, that it was standing straight up. Almost the way it looks after you've been jumping on a trampoline, only we weren't. We were walking down a street off of Times Square. We looked around, wide-eyed, our jaws dropped over the weirdness of it all. Because it was just us. It was just that spot. And it was somehow charged with enough static electricity to make it look like we were putting our hands on one of those static-charged balls at a museum.

A few steps more and we were out of it, the static vortex, and so we stepped right back into it and laughed as hysterically as I'd laughed in a long time. This is the scene I remember when I think of seeing *Newsies* on Broadway. I think of how new laughter felt after heartbreak, and of being reminded that there is a great big world out there beyond this single person who once loved you. I remember that the tears I shed that night were from hysteria, in a good way, and I remember feeling comforted in the knowledge that friendships outlast all the relationships you'll ever have.

The relationship I was pining the loss of had some threads of Broadway woven into it, including tickets to a production of *Once*. It was the first day that things were beginning to re-open after Hurricane Sandy had blown through, and we attended a Wednesday matinee. A delightful show with its undertones of longing and constant blend of Irish jigs, I was most affected by the number that closed the first act. "Gold," it was called.

And I love her so, I wouldn't trade her for gold.

Sitting there next to my boyfriend, it felt like the song was being sung about us. That it could have been him saying those words about me. I saw the show again after he broke up with me the following year, and this time those words tore apart some inner piece of me. Because he *had* traded me. For what I wasn't completely sure, but whatever it was felt like a hell of a lot less than gold. And was I worth so little? By the time the song ended that second time around and the lights came up for intermission, I was sobbing hysterical, guttural sobs. And loudly.

I had to go a third round with the show, to prove to myself that I had conquered the whole experience, and so around Christmastime I treated myself and two of my friends, Molly included, to one of the show's final performances on Broadway. I was getting ready to quit my job and felt like it was my last chance to splurge. My friends both made far less money than I did, and almost as satisfying as seeing their grateful glee was getting through "Gold" with dry eyes.

It's those kinds of things that get to me, though. Simple, really. Like how I can't hear ABBA without wanting to dance, without thinking about my Aunt Leah flying in on the redeye for a weekend in the city with me, without feeling the way we felt that night as we stood and waved our arms to the closing bonus numbers the *Mamma Mia* cast sang, without knowing I love her so much and forever. It's what taught me that the people who are meant to be with you won't trade you for anything. Period. That is what theater can do, any night of the week.

Except Monday, apparently.

SIDEBAR: SERVICE IN THE CITY AND SEEING INTO MY FUTURE

There's a Manhattan-based organization called DOROT that facilitates care and companionship of the city's elderly population. Generations helping generations, that's their slogan. It's not that I sought them out, although living in New York City does make a person think about what will be the state of things if you're *still* living in New York City fifty or sixty years from now.

Or maybe the real crux is whether you'll still be *single* and living in New York City fifty or sixty years from now.

Or maybe it's whether you'll be single and still living in the same *walk-up apartment* in New York City fifty or sixty years from now.

At any rate, it doesn't take long as a New Yorker to realize

that it can be a real bitch of a place for those with health ailments, those who have a hard time getting around, who are lonely, who are losing their sight, their ability to control their bowels, their directional certitude. In short, the elderly. So when my church congregation asked for volunteers to spend a Sunday delivering care packages for DOROT, it struck me as something that was very needed in this city. If that would be me in fifty or sixty years, or even if it wouldn't, I wanted to help.

DOROT is a Jewish organization, but you don't have to be Jewish to volunteer, so I took the subway over to the West Side on my assigned Sunday morning to receive some initial training. Most emphatically impressed upon me, *Mission Impossible* style, was the repeated mandate that the piece of paper with the address of the elderly person I was to visit must be destroyed in such a way that no one could ever find it or decipher it. Nor was I to be able to so much as *remember* the address myself after my initial visit.* After being paired with an elderly lady who lived on the East Side, I schlepped the care package down into the subway and examined its contents while speeding downtown in ten-block increments.

The bag contained mostly canned or boxed food items. Some things I recognized, like beans. Some things I didn't, like Jewish things that I wasn't sure how to pronounce. There was some literature in the bag as well—warm wishes for the upcoming holiday, tips for keeping safe in the winter, etc. All in all this seemed like such a lovely thing for an organization to be doing.

It became less lovely when the subway was delayed and I didn't get to the woman's building within the time I'd told her I would. And less lovely still when I finally arrived and buzzed the apartment and she no longer even wanted me to come up. I negotiated from the lobby that even if she was no longer up for a visit, she should at least let me drop the care package. She reluctantly agreed.

---

*Um, okay?

One of the shortest elevator rides I can recall, before I was the least bit ready I was knocking on this woman's door. I was prepared to dislike her greatly as she looked me up and down from the bed in the center of her room.

"Well, you're obviously not Jewish," she said.

And she had me. With that one line, I knew we would get along.

My subsequent visits went much better, and each time I volunteered with DOROT I requested this woman, Evelyn was her name, and each time I schlepped her bag of food and Jewish paraphernalia from a high school on the Upper West Side to a dingy apartment building on the Lower East Side.* Oddly, I never once saw her look inside the bag, nor did she ever inquire as to its contents. Apparently that was not what she looked forward to about my visits. From the moment I walked in, Evelyn held my eye, asked me questions, answered mine, and it almost pained me that this was all the exposure she likely got to genuine, interesting people. Or *any* people.

This is DOROT's main mission, this kind of companionship, and aside from these relatively low-touch occasional visits, a volunteer can be as involved as she wants to be. You can do everything from help an elderly New Yorker complete his grocery shopping to attend a Broadway show with an elderly person who has no one to go with. It's about whatever the person needs, and I could make myself teary with gratitude when thinking about DOROT's recognition that having a theater buddy is a very real need.

Theater wasn't really in the picture for Evelyn, who lived

---

*Or maybe it wasn't. Maybe it was somewhere else. I forgot as instructed.

in the hospital bed in the center of her bedroom, unable to leave her apartment. Unable to walk, really. She lived with a beautiful cat, an Abyssinian, clearly devoted to her. She need only call out, "Kitty! Kitty!" for the creature to appear in her lap from some obscure corner. It could have struck me as sad, this spinster woman and her cat. I was certainly headed in that same direction. But instead it buoyed me up that they had each other; that a cat will bond with its owner regardless of her age or physical condition.

Evelyn had spent her career in the movie business. Not in front of the cameras, but behind them. Cinematography, if that's what they called it back then, and she must have spent hours telling me stories about famous Hollywood actors and actresses. Julie Andrews, Shirley MacClaine. I wish I'd written it all down right away, because I've already forgotten which ones she said were wonderful, which ones were rude, and which was the one who finally told off a costume guy who always said inappropriate things to the actresses. Because doesn't that seem important somehow? Knowing these things? Shouldn't this kind of firsthand account be preserved?

She seemed equally fascinated by my study of gemology, and one afternoon saw her directing me to a little box on a desk across the room.

"Bring it to me," she said when I'd pointed to the right box.

It was filled with jewelry. All the baubles she'd collected over a very long lifetime. None of them had any monetary value, but still, there were stories. People. Relatives. There were loves. All represented in the heap of color now sifting through a pair of wrinkled hands.

This would be me, I thought. *Surrounded by my cat and my jewels.*

The last time I visited Evelyn, she asked if I would bring with me some of the gemstones I was studying on my next visit. It was an easy request, as I always had gems at my apartment, on loan from school as a part of my training, of course. I thought I'd bring her the opal. Or maybe the rhodochrosite—the piece I had looked just like bacon with its wriggly pink lines. But I never made it back to Evelyn's apartment. I ended up getting a job offer much sooner than expected. A gemology job, one that would take me across the country to the west coast before I'd had a chance to visit Evelyn again.

And of all the things moving suddenly from a place leaves untied—leases broken, new furniture unused, event tickets wasted—the thing that kept me up at night was Evelyn.

Because what if she wondered where I was? What if DOROT called to schedule her next delivery and she expected me on the other side of the door? What if she was distracted thinking about gemstones while some girl who probably *would* look Jewish talked her ear off about the elementary school kids she taught across town? What if she felt I'd let her down by not being there?

And so I wrote Evelyn a letter. I copied her address from the printout I was supposed to have destroyed.* Even though I had no idea if she would get it, if she could read it, or if she would even care about my future life as a gemologist, mailing that letter—in the midst of the moving chaos—was the one thing I was sure about. It was what I could do.

---

*Somewhere Tom Cruise is shaking his head.

I looked Evelyn up on IMDB, just because I was curious, and while her entry is short, she *is* listed. With credits to many movies, including big ones, like *Bridge on the River Kwai*. I think about her sometimes, her career and her cat and her clutter surrounding that hospital bed. I wish so much for her, for the end of her life, for those final years or months or weeks when maybe she knew the end was near. Because what even goes through a person's head at that point? *Who will take care of Kitty? Who will know that I have died? And whatever happened to that girl who promised she'd bring over an opal?*

GOING

IT ONLY TOOK A FEW DAYS FOR MY LANDLORDS
to take pity on me and switch my gassy oven—the one that
either stank constantly or required that I light the pilot light
each time I wanted to cook—for their normal one, the kind
that had gas burners that simply ignited when you turned
the knobs and shut off when you turned them back the other
way, and it made a world of difference. But I still wouldn't
say I *cooked*.

I'd had grand ambitions to cook, mind you; to look out at
the fall crispness you could almost see as it gradually stripped
the trees of their leaves while my quiches and apple pies baked.
But truthfully, it just wasn't feasible. The oven itself couldn't
even accommodate a regular-sized baking sheet or casserole
dish. It was, I was fairly certain, the smallest oven ever made.

And even if I found pans and sheets small enough to fit inside, I still only had about twelve inches of counter space. So it was hard to imagine tackling a pie when I didn't even have room to roll out the dough. Nor did I own a rolling pin. Or a pie pan. Or have room for things like flour. OK, *so just forget the pie.*

The point I'm trying to make is that baking became a rarity, something I really only attempted with logs of frozen cookie dough. I'd buy it from the grocery store around the corner and slice four cookies' worth and place them on my tiny baking sheet. I'd then relish in the satisfaction of *baking* in New York City; of something actually being produced by my tiny oven; of the smell of butter and sugar and chocolate being as familiar in this environment than in any other. Indeed, waiting for chocolate chip cookies to come out of the oven is oddly one of my happiest and most vivid memories of fall nights in New York.

If you call this ambitious, which I don't, then you could say I tackled cooking with equal ambition, never straying from that which could be heated or boiled on one of my small range burners. It was part practicality, as I simply did not have the space or resources to add complexity to my meals, but it was also partly due to the cost of food, which is something I hadn't seen coming.

True that *everything* costs more in New York City, with the exception of dry cleaning and Brazilian waxes, but the markup on food, particularly produce, was staggering. The non-sale price of an avocado in my neighborhood grocery store was $4.99. That's for one avocado. I quickly decided produce in general would have to be scrapped from my diet, a decision I stuck to unless I found a cheap street produce vendor and happened to have cash on me. Which was basically never, because despite what you always hear about how you should never be caught in the city without cash, the only people requiring cash payment are street vendors, dry cleaners, and the homeless.

A typical shopping trip, usually to the local grocer once a week, would yield something like this:

> Pasta noodles – whatever was on sale
> Canned pasta sauce – whatever was on sale
> Ramen noodle packs
> Cup o Noodles
> Spaghettios
> Ravioli
> A few baking potatoes
> Ranch powder seasoning
> Liquid eggs
> Tortillas
> Log of cookie dough
> Tortilla chips
> Salsa
> Fancy Feast for the cat

What should shock you is how unhealthy this diet is, as well as how much it resembles (read: is verbatim the same thing as) the diet we all subsisted on in college. It was a complete reincarnation of the *Things You Eat When You Don't Cook and Have No Money Anyway Diet*. Even as a gainfully employed corporate professional, I was adjusting to a cost of living that was two-and-a-half times more than what I'd experienced in Cleveland. I simply had to budget. And what I ate was something I could control. The most maddening part of it all was that as soon as you left the city, prices dropped. My brother and sister-in-law lived in New Jersey, about an hour train ride from Penn Station, and I brought an extra suitcase each time I visited so that I could stuff it with groceries.

I did learn ways to shop cheap, one of them being those street produce vendors, but I'm a little ashamed to admit that my diet never strayed very far from that shopping list. I cooked simply, I ate cheaply, and despite the lack of nutritional value in my diet as well as the frequency of treats like Carnegie Deli cheesecake and Serendipity frozen hot chocolate, I managed to be the only girl I knew who moved to New York City and lost weight. Looking back, it makes me sad. It makes me sad that I curbed my diet because I was worried about money. It makes me sad that I didn't tackle cooking in earnest. And it's probably a word worse than sad that I scrapped produce but kept my Brazilian waxes.

I live in California now, and every time I slice an avocado over a piece of toast, it feels like luxury. So does having a toaster.

COMING

AT SOME POINT DURING MY MONTHS OF studying gems in New York City, my sister, who has a knack for giving perfect gifts, mailed me a soft, blue t-shirt that said this: *Don't Quit Your Day Dream*. It was the most inspiring sentiment I'd ever heard, and I knew as soon as I saw it that I wanted to be wearing this shirt when I passed my big final test. I got it out on the morning of my first attempt and put it on, realizing my wardrobe plan might prove tricky since passing on the first try wasn't exactly realistic. So...what? I'd wear the shirt all week?

My friend Molly predicted I'd pass on the first try. So did my dad. And hearing them say this over the days and weeks leading up to the test had filled me with a kind of rage I'm rather embarrassed to admit. They meant is as a compliment—they believed in me, they knew how hard I'd been working, they were trying to give me confidence—but I found it offensive. For them to predict something that was simply not possible infuriated me. It meant I'd have to go back to them with news of failure and disprove their theory that I was ready, that I was *that* talented, that I was capable of success right off the bat. They simply didn't understand what I was up against.

I was listening to music while walking the few blocks from the subway to campus on the morning of my first attempt, headphones in, oblivious to horns and voices and sirens. The song that came on in that moment was from the animated movie *Anastasia** and began with words that seemed hand-picked for the day.

> *Heart don't fail me now,*
> *Courage don't desert me,*
> *Don't turn back now that we're here.*
> *People always say,*
> *Life is full of choices,*
> *No one ever mentions fear.*

By the time the song wound to its conclusion, I was staring up at the towering campus building that hovered over 47th Street. I was nervous, but it was there. And inside was the desk I would sit in, the stones I would identify. Inside was my instructor waiting, the security guards that printed me a new badge each day even though it seemed like something I should be able to reuse. I knew this place, and I

---

*No judgement, please.

knew these stones, so why was it so hard to allow myself even the smallest amount of confidence?

Yes, let this be a sign,
Let this road be mine,
Let it lead me to my past,
And bring me home at last.

So, not *exactly* the same situation. This was more about finding my future than seeking out the past that had been stolen from me. But still. You listen to that song and tell me if that ending doesn't leave you feeling inspired and more capable of facing *anything* you've got coming at you.

Once checked in and settled into my spot in the front row of the student laboratory, my instructor approached carrying a large bin. Inside were about a dozen boxes of stones, and I was to pick one. This action struck me as incredibly crucial, in that these boxes were all different. They contained different stones. And some of the boxes, based on my own strengths and weaknesses as a budding gemologist, would undoubtedly be boxes I could not successfully pass. Some of them contained stones that would inevitably stump me.

I didn't fish around or go for the bottom. I took the box on the top left, the one closest to me.

I drew a breath, sat down, and opened it.

I didn't scan the box to see what I'd gotten. I simply took out the first stone, polished it, and began making notes on my worksheet. By lunchtime I had worked my way through half of the box, and what I remember most about the morning of that first attempt is how calm I felt once I started examining the stones. Because this was so familiar to me by then. And even though any one of those little suckers could ultimately cost me a passing grade, each gem was so exceptionally unique and beautiful. I just *loved* this. *Don't quit your day dream.* Only one of the morning's stones gave me any pause. A dark green cabochon, it was clearly either jadeite or nephrite, which are both varieties of jade. They're both green, but jadeite is typically more green, and nephrite commonly contains brown overtones. Their numbers on the refractive index are not identical, but very close. As I examined the stone, it looked more like jadeite, but its numbers were slightly lower than I would have expected for that stone. I reasoned that more evidence pointed to nephrite and wrote it down, in pencil, on my worksheet.

Getting up to go to lunch at the halfway point of the test, my instructor called after me as I moved to exit the lab.

"Tali, what are you doing?"

"Going to lunch."

"You have to hand in your test first."

"But I'm only halfway done."

"Yes, you turn in the first half now."

This I had not expected. It's not so much that I was planning to noodle over the jadeite/nephrite dilemma over a deli grilled cheese and tomato sandwich, even though I was. It's that I could have already failed. Half of my answers would now be submitted, officially. Yet even if something was already wrong, I still had to come back and take the second half of the test. It seemed a cruel trick for someone in the grading room to know this and not tell me until the test was fully completed. If I hadn't chosen correctly on the jadeite/nephrite, or on anything else, what a waste my afternoon would be.

JADEITE, NEPHRITE.
JADEITE, NEPHRITE.
JADEITE, NEPHRITE.

It felt like a heartbeat, like a train clack, something both rhythmic and unavoidable as I finished lunch and walked back to campus, through security, up the elevators, down the hall, into the lab, and reached my seat to face the second half of my box of stones.

The surprising calm settled in once again as I resumed working, pausing only once to waffle over whether a ruby was natural or synthetic. I concluded synthetic, even though it didn't have the typical inclusions seen in a synthetic ruby. It's more that it just didn't look natural.

I had until 4:00 to finish the test, but at some point in the afternoon I realized that all my worksheet fields were filled in. All my answers were complete.

I held out my worksheet and let the paper slip from my hand into my instructor's.

While he took the worksheet down the hall to be graded, I went to the restroom to wash any toxic refractive index fluid remnants off my hands. As I did, I looked at myself in the mirror, wearing the soft blue t-shirt, and paused for a moment. I felt inklings of what I can only describe as confidence. And a short sentence came to mind as I looked myself in the eye, water dripping from my hands. *I just may have done this.*

It seemed absurd, but just maybe.

Back in my seat in the lab, my instructor came through

the door with my two graded worksheets stapled together. He was looking me right in the eye, his gaze unwavering as he approached. His expression wasn't happy, but it wasn't sad either. It wasn't pity or excitement. Not pride or disappointment. The only thing I could identify in his eyes was intensity, and maybe a little bit of urgency. He simply handed me the papers, which were marked on the score line with an underlined "*100 percent.*"

I'd thought if I passed on the first try that I'd cry, because who *does* that? Because I had worked so hard. Because there was so much riding on this. Because it was my dream. Instead I put my head in my hands and laughed, letting out something super mature like, "No way!" Because it was honestly so hard to believe. There was a girl on the next aisle on her third or fourth attempt, and she was only getting worse, missing five today. I felt almost bad sitting there celebrating with my instructor, a near expressionless, no-nonsense man who was obviously impressed.

"On the first try," he was saying. "Now that's something to be proud of."

"This was the last thing I needed. I'm done with all the coursework."

"Then you're officially a Graduate Gemologist," he said. "Congratulations."

It felt almost anticlimactic, in that there was no celebration of sorts, no party, no official ceremony or pomp. There was just me and my instructor, a few students finishing up various assignments, and the perfect worksheets still in my hand.

And then there was this, from the stoic man who had taught nearly all of my courses.

"After watching you and the way you prepared for this," my instructor said, "I have no doubt that you'll be able to accomplish anything you set your mind to."

And it's one of those things I've held onto. One of those things an educator says that shapes you, propels you forward, and leaves you feeling the same except for the slightly perceptible change that is an additional person on your side. They make a difference, those shifts and propulsions. And rarely does a day go by where I don't think about this instructor, now retired, and his belief in me and my abilities. The look in his eye when he wanted so badly for me to know I had passed but wanted even more for me to see it for myself on the top of the paper.

Getting off at 110th Street, I went straight to Molly's. We celebrated in Central Park as she took a few pictures of me, in the soft blue t-shirt and unable to stop smiling. I'm not sure what I was really wanting to capture. It's just that we get so few perfect days in our lives. So few instances of things working out just the way we hope and plan. So few opportunities to achieve our longest and most closely-held dreams. And even if no one else knows when looking at those pictures, me in a pixie cut twirling around a lamppost, it's enough for me to know that on this particular day, all of that happened.

Don't quit your day dream.

Not ever.

GOING

THE NIGHT BEFORE THE MOVE, I WAS IN A surreal sort of haze. I'd lived in Cleveland for almost seven years. The longest I'd lived anywhere in my adult life. Really, it's the *only* place I'd lived outside of where I either grew up or attended college and graduate school. My little Cleveland house on my little Cleveland street in my little Cleveland suburb. The place where I became a professional, rescued my cat, fell in love, and acquired scars from both a muscle biopsy* and from that love falling to pieces in the eleventh hour.

Even being relatively removed from the romantic relationship at that point, in that it had been some time, I still felt wrapped up in it. It weighed on me. Not in a painful

---

*"I wish *my* thighs looked like that," I heard one of the nurses say just before the anesthesia took hold.

way, not anymore. But in a way that, at the very least, had me acutely aware of the fact that the most important thing I was leaving behind in this city was what might have been had this man not decided that he couldn't marry me. It still felt like a lot to have lost, and it's partly why I'd been crafting my final pre-move social media post for months, and why rolling the words over in my mind would always make me tear up. That night I posted them and felt a kind of finality that I can only describe as both gloriously freeing and achingly lonely.

My last night in Cleveland. So grateful to everyone who has been a part of these years. The good, the bad, and the heartbreaking. I have been bettered by being here.

I no longer had a bed to sleep in, which my ex's sister, single and my age, had noticed when she stopped by my empty house. She'd offered to help me with any last-minute moving tasks, and while I'm sure she was horrified when she realized that the boxes in the basement that I asked her to break down represented nearly seven years' worth of me throwing virtually every corrugated container I'd received down the stairs to deal with at a later date, she took a breath in and rolled up her sleeves and broke down every one of those boxes. Then she came back upstairs and surveyed my empty house.

"Where are you sleeping tonight?" she asked.

I pointed to my little air mattress in the corner.

"No, you're not," she said. "You're staying with us."

And I wanted to cry. Over the generosity of a family who had no reason to still embrace me in this way. This same sister had helped me work my garage sale the previous weekend, and in the slow lulls between selling off my books and stemware and picture frames, we would talk. Not so much about her brother, although it did come up. At that point his family didn't know how he'd left things (he left them pretty shitty) and I wasn't strong enough to talk about the fact that he'd decided the best way to handle ending things was to just never talk to me again.

"I don't know how a person does that," was all I could say. "How do you do that to someone?"

Standing across from me in my narrow, possession-strewn driveway in Cleveland, my ex's sister didn't answer my question, but she had tears in her eyes. I know she cared for me—they all did. But they cared for him, too. And they were bound by blood. They probably should have been circling their wagons around him, and instead they were breaking down boxes in my basement and manning the cash box at my garage sale. And at the end of each day, his parents would show up to help, and they, along with me and his sister, would carry in the tables and box up the odds and ends to be laid out again the following day.

So maybe it was inevitable that my last night in Cleveland would see me bathed in their goodness once more. No family had been a bigger part of my time in Cleveland, and in some sort of sick way that probably makes sense to my therapist, their closeness was comforting to me. Not because of my ex, but because I had relationships with each of them independent of him. They mattered to me. Far away from my own, they were shining examples of a functional, intact, and caring family that had for a time made me a part of it all.

It would be another three years after I moved before

my ex, a new girlfriend in the picture, told them he was no longer comfortable with this closeness. While it's not exactly inappropriate to continue to see your ex's family when you come to town, it's probably not *appropriate* either. So I shouldn't have been shocked three years post move to suddenly get the cold shoulder when on my way to Cleveland for a visit. Once I realized they were united in this front, that they had circled their wagons around him after all, I locked myself in an airport bathroom and sobbed uncontrollably. Not because of him. I'd lost him years ago. But *them*. I'd had them all along, and losing them felt a little like losing Cleveland. Like something deep in my innards had been irreversibly severed.

Of course, I didn't know any of this on that last night in Cleveland as I fell asleep in his parents' house, my cat hiding under the bed for fear of her unknown surroundings, bits of litter from her makeshift box now buried in the shaggy carpet of what may have been my ex's childhood room. I only knew that I owed them a lot. And I wished I could have said as much when they hugged me in their kitchen the next day. It had to have been 4:00 in the morning, them in their bathrobes to see me off, and his sister loaded me and my cat into the car and drove us away before I could really process, let alone articulate, any kind of goodbye.

On the Manhattan end of the trip, in a taxi on the way to my new apartment, I received a message from my ex. A funny article he'd found about ways to cope with living in New York City. The article made me smile, or maybe what made me smile was that we were broken up but not broken.

On a crowded city street, waiting for a light to turn, in

no one's company but a muttering, foreign taxi driver and my drugged-up cat still loopy from the meds I'd given her,[*] I typed out a reply that contained the crux of what I had been meaning to say all along.

"Take care of that family of yours. They have been so kind to me. I don't deserve it, but I'll never forget it."

His reply came swiftly.

"The notion that you don't deserve it is ridiculous. I can't think of anyone who deserves it more."

I didn't reply again, figuring that was as good an ending to our chapter as any.

Plus my cat had started drooling on the taxi seat.

---

[*]Clearly you've never seen the highly-acclaimed and utterly horrifying *Cats on a Plane*.

Sidebar: Pets in Manhattan and How My Cat Learned to Sleep

As a long-time cat owner, I've noticed people tend to think you're being ridiculous when you at all insinuate that your cat is as, or more, important to you than most *people*. It's true that I'm particularly devoted to my cat and get a little sparkly-eyed when talking about her, but in defense of single cat owners everywhere, let's consider the facts.

There's really only one, and it's that she's the only other living thing in your house.

She's the only one who depends on you for life, for sustenance. The only one waiting for you when you get home, missing you while you're gone, curling up in your lap when you cry, and settling in as an eager listener to every guitar concert, even though you only ever play the same five songs.

So yes, I am *that* pet owner. The one who calls her

veterinarian father at the slightest change in behavior and asks the cat sitter to send pictures. The one who buys shirts that say things like "I work hard so my cat can have a better life." Because I do. And she does. I make no apologies for this. It is simply a fact that there is something different about the bond that forms between pet and owner when there aren't any other people in the house. When she's all you've got.

This is all to say that I wondered while living in New York if the move had affected my cat's quality of life.

Most notably, there was the difference in size between our previous home and our new studio apartment. In Cleveland, where I'd adopted her, she had free reign of 1,200 square feet on two stories. She had several more rooms to inhabit, to find nooks and crannies in which to warm herself come winter. On one hand, it felt a bit cruel that she was now reduced to such a small amount of space, but on the other hand, she spent most of the day sleeping. Did she really need all those rooms?

I figured the biggest drawback to the lack of space must have been the consequent lack of windows. Each of the studio apartments we lived in during our time in Manhattan only had one window. So while she probably got along just fine in the smaller space, I did feel badly that each apartment now only offered one view. *The courtyard? Again?*

Between the lack of both space and windows, I started taking the cat outside of the apartment. Never to the extent of those walking their cats around the neighborhood on a leash,* but I did get one. A leash. I'd put it on the cat and

---

*Something about this never seemed quite right to me...probably because *IT'S CRAZY.*

lead her out into the third-floor hallway. I always expected her to be a little more interested in poking around, going up and down the stairs, sniffing. But she never went very far and always seemed uncomfortable. As if she just wanted to get back inside the tiny apartment in which she'd been cooped up all day. All week. All month.

Once I even took her up to the roof, a lovely view at five stories high. She didn't like it, shaking in my arms as I walked us over to the edge to take in the beauty of the late fall afternoon. The leash didn't get much use after that, which I don't think either of us minded.

Another difference between Cleveland and New York was that I no longer had an actual bedroom to shut her out of each night when I wanted to sleep. Always more active at night, she'd jump up on the bed and pounce on my feet under the covers as I was trying to drift off. In Cleveland I took to tossing one of her fake mice down the stairs, watching her barrel down after it, and then shutting the door to get some sleep. She never meowed or scratched, she just did whatever she did at night and was always happy to greet me when I emerged the following morning.

In New York there was no way for me to separate us at bedtime. We had to exist in the same space. While it took some time, if there's one thing New York did for us, it's that it got my cat to finally sleep at the same time I did. She began climbing up onto my loft bed in our Harlem apartment and curling up at my feet to sleep. Which is what I had always hoped she would do. Even after leaving New York and moving west and once again having an actual bedroom, I still don't close the door. Because she gets it.

Of course I worried while living on the Upper East Side that the cat would develop a complex, some sort of stress disorder from the woman downstairs always brooming the ceiling up at us. Surely she heard it and made the correlation between her movement and the obscenities being shouted up from below. And she had to be affected by my temporarily shutting her in the bathroom at night to keep her from bothering the woman. Eventually I wised up to the fact that the only one stressing out about the bitch downstairs was me. Still, when we moved to Harlem and the man below us didn't give a rat's ass when my cat ran around above him, I felt something beyond relief, something almost parental, in that I had provided a much healthier environment for the one living thing for which I was responsible.

Look, I'm not an idiot. I know she won't always be here, this darling cat who has been my companion for almost a decade. I know at some point I'll lose her, and I know that this loss will not be the same as a human one. And while the image I'll most often picture is me holding her for the first time at an animal shelter in east Cleveland, knowing she was mine just from that, my mind will also turn to the image of a striped cat perched on the sill of a sunny third-floor window, staring out at the buildings across the street, wanting for absolutely nothing.

COMING

WHEN MY FRIEND SAID HE WANTED ME TO MEET the B-list celebrity he'd been dating,* I was all in. And by that I mean I was a total fame-stalking freak about it. That's just how I am. When it comes to celebrities, I have absolutely zero shame. The chance to meet someone I've seen on TV or in movies? Someone who lives a life completely foreign to mine? Someone who doesn't have to work a 9:00 to 5:00 office job just to get by? If only MORE of my friends would briefly date and then hang onto awkward friendships with celebrities.

This celebrity, who'd achieved pretty wide notoriety many years before through being the runner up on a popular

---

*Or maybe they were already over and had settled on just being friends...I was never quite sure of the nature of their relationship.

reality singing competition, lived in Manhattan, as did I. The plan was for me to—wait for it—GO TO HIS APART-MENT and then he would drive us, like in his own car, over to the Bronx where my friend lived.

It shocked me when I saw from his address that this celebrity lived in Harlem, only nine blocks away from me. He was on Central Park North in a very nice building, mind you, but still. To think I'd been living here in such close proximity to him. To think that we might frequent the same ghetto grocery store on the corner (doubtful) or that I might run into him at my favorite local pizza joint or bakery (probably even more doubtful) was thrilling. *Our hood, yo.*

The thought occurred to me as I walked the nine blocks to his apartment building on the appointed morning that if his place of residence was widely known, maybe all kinds of crazies were showing up asking for him at the desk in the lobby. What if the attendant didn't believe me?

"I'm supposed to meet B. Celebrity here?" I said more like a question than a statement when I reached the man sitting at the desk.

I'd used his real name, and I learned later that most celebrities, including B., have fake names that they give when needed, such that asking for a celebrity by their fake name becomes a password of sorts. If you know the fake name, you're obviously legit. Yet somehow even with the real name I'd given, the man at the desk still picked up the phone and called B. Celebrity, who'd of course been expecting me. Within a few minutes he strode through the lobby, a smile on his face.

"Tali?" he asked with a bit of an accent, his hand extended for me to shake.

And without further ado, he led us into the building's garage where we got into his car—a nice car but not a crazy nice car—and began winding through the streets of Harlem, bound for the Bronx. I remember almost nothing of this conversation, mostly because my head was running a near-constant reel that went something like, *"You're in the car with B. Celebrity. B. Celebrity is sitting right next to you. You will be spending the day with B. Celebrity. You could reach out and touch B. Celebrity. But don't. Be cool."*

Picking up our friend at his home in the Bronx, the three of us then headed over to the Botanical Gardens for the day. And it's an interesting thing, being out in public with a celebrity. On one hand, I kept thinking no one would notice. I mean, he was B-list, remember? It's not like I was walking around with Angelina Jolie. But the thing was, *everyone* noticed. *Everyone* recognized him. People talked to him on the tram, approached him on the walking paths, even the manager of the restaurant where we lunched brought out free food simply because he recognized B. Celebrity.

It was all rather impressive. And by that I mean I was crazy hot with jealousy. I wanted his life. Or at least I wanted free dessert when I dined out.

What was also impressive was B. Celebrity's ability to handle each encounter with a grace that acknowledged the fan's having recognized him and thanked them for their compliments yet also minimized the spectacle of it all. He had a way, clearly crafted over years of being a recognizable figure, of responding to someone in a hushed, low-key way that discouraged both a congregation of additional fans as well as an overall disturbance in the establishment. I admired that in him. And I admired how devoted his fans were.

"I'm from PARTICULAR STATE as well!" one said enthusiastically, and they chatted for a quiet moment about where the eager gentleman was from.

"I voted for you so many times!" said another, and B. thanked him for the support.

The gardens were beautiful on this particular day in late spring, and the whole atmosphere of appreciating the beauty of the world around us had me and B. waxing Disney. We'd gotten started in the car, discussing our favorite Disney songs and singing along as loud as we could to such classics as "Be a Man" and "Out There."

"There really aren't very many epic Disney songs for men," B. said.

"What about "Go the Distance?" I asked, to which he immediately pulled out his phone.

"I forgot about that one! I'm texting my manager."

He'd recently had a gig performing Disney songs and couldn't believe he had forgotten it.

We sang it right there in the car. Me and B. Celebrity. As loud as we could.

> *I am ooooooooon my waaaaaaaaaay,*
> *I can goooooooooo the distance.*
> *I don't caaaaaaaaare how faaaaaaaaaaar,*
> *Somehow I'll be stroooooooong.*
> *I know eeeeeeevery miiiiiiiiile*

Will be wooooooooooorth my whiiiiiiiiiile.
I would goooooo most anywheeeeeeeeeere
to fiiiiiiiiind where IIIIIIIIIIIIII
belooooooooooooooooooooooooooong.

In the gardens, my friend recorded B. and me singing "Colors of the Wind" and B. then streamed it on his social media pages. A part of me did think this may be my moment; that I really ought to be in audition mode, convincing B. that recording a duet with me was clearly his next professional venture. Or at least letting me ghost write his memoir.

As we continued through the gardens, the live streams kept coming, a series of video clips that his manager ultimately described on his website the next day as an outing "with friends Tali Nay and Patrick Barnes," which got me a healthy influx of Twitter followers. They've all since abandoned me after learning that this was a one-time deal, but the momentary attention made me feel, for lack of a better word, important. Just me, having a fun day, out on the town, with my celebrity friend. As you do.

We went from the gardens to dinner at an Indian restaurant, where B. continued to be recognized by almost everyone there, including the managing staff. And after dropping our friend off at his house at the end of the day, B. then drove us back to Harlem. I was days away from moving, California-bound, and I expressed to B. in the fading evening light how nervous I was to drive out of the city in what would be my rental car. For people who don't drive in the city, it can seem cripplingly intimidating, and I had real anxiety about navigating my way off of the island.

"I'd be happy to drive you if that makes you less stressed about it," he offered, rather surprisingly.

What, to California? Get. Out.

"What do you mean?" I asked after hallucinating for a second.

"As in I'll drive you out of the city, Patrick following behind, and then I'll hand it back to you and jump in with him."

The gesture disarmed me, because I didn't really know B. I'd just met him, sang a few songs with him, shot the shit with him mostly while thinking that he was a bit of a diva. And here he was offering what to me was no small thing.

I knew there was no way I could let him do it, but I was genuinely touched. And I'd learned something from B. He'd been surprisingly honest after hearing about my gemology endeavors. I'd just passed my big test and was about to start my new job, my first in the gemology industry, and I was a little sad (read: completely depressed) about having to say goodbye to the delightful world of Not Having a Day Job. When I said as much to B., he confessed that the downside of not having a day job is having nothing to do. Now, see, isn't that interesting? He was *complaining about having nothing to do.*

"Having just experienced a phase of life where I had no job and no responsibilities, it was pretty much the best thing ever," I said.

"Yeah, but you were still working toward being a gemologist. You had a goal," he said.

I'd say it's the classic case of the grass always being greener, it's just that celebrity grass always seems like it's the greenest. Let's not forget, the man gets *paid* to sing Disney songs. So what gives? Was B. actually a little bit jealous of my regular-person life? At least parts of it? I believe he was, and it made me feel good inside. I was never going to be famous, but I'd settle for knowing that there are aspects of my life that are enviable even to those who appear to have it all. I'd settle for a day about town with a B-list celebrity, both of us singing in his car at the top of our lungs. I'd settle for that evening drive back into the city, the skyline lights before us, and the way he said "Tali, *sing* girl!" when I hit Pocahontas' high note.

Sidebar: New Yorkers and Where They Live

Before moving to New York, my exposure to New Yorkers was limited to the owners of the apartments I rented through Airbnb when vacationing.

It had taken me a while to even *get* to the point of using Airbnb. Hotels have always just seemed so *sexy* to me. Something about their temporary nature, about the fact that you come back each night to find fresh linens and all your crap organized neatly on the polished bathroom counter. And there's something about room service, about points that accumulate to give you more perks the next time you stay.

Of course, the sexiest thing about staying at a hotel is when someone else is paying the bill. A friend once described a company-paid business trip as feeling like Christmas morning, and I knew exactly what she meant. You come home to a nice, clean hotel room each night, a bigger and more comfortable bed than the one you have at home. You wake up to the call of a friendly desk clerk, roll down to the gym you're not paying for and the Starbucks you can charge to per diem, and get ready for the day while watching channels you're too cheap to pay for at home. And it's costing you *nothing*?*

This was fine for work trips, but many of my New York City trips were vacations and, hence, on my own dime. And at some point I wised up to the fact that Airbnb—staying in an actual New Yorker's apartment—was usually cheaper. And even when it wasn't, even when the cost was the same, there were some added perks. Like being able to store and prepare food and being able to have a more genuine experience. To essentially try the life of a New Yorker on for size. Sleeping in their beds, using their toilets, walking up and down the stairs of their buildings. As someone who had a crush on the whole big, beautiful island, the idea completely charmed me.

The first apartment I rented was right off of Times Square. In the thick of 46th Street, between a steakhouse and an Irish pub, was a door that led up to a few apartments. A door you could have walked by a dozen times and never even noticed amid the noise and bustle of the tourist-heavy passersby. It just wasn't the sort of block you'd expect people to live on. But that's the thing about New York City. People live on *every* block.

The apartment was sparsely furnished and appeared to function solely as a vacation rental. There were no belongings, no real evidence of an owner or occupant, but I still wondered. Because who *did* own this place? Did they ever come here? Spend an occasional day or weekend soaking in the sights and sounds of these streets? I thought these things as I tried to sleep at night in one of the apartment's two tiny

---

*There are many downsides to the company-paid business trip as well, but that's for another book.

makeshift bedrooms, not even minding the saturated cigarette smell that overpowered the apartment or the constant
barrage of noise outside, because I was in *Manhattan*. I was
in Times Square, in the thick of it.

My choice the next time I came to town was a square-
shaped studio a bit more removed from Times Square. It was
off of 8th Avenue, if I recall, somewhere around 55th Street, and
unlike my first rental, this apartment was actually the owner's
home. Books filled the shelves, clothes lined the closets. It
was almost bursting, in that containing an entire human life
and its acquired possessions in a single room is difficult.

The owner was a short, Asian man in his thirties, whom
I assumed was gay. Both because he *seemed* gay and because
he mentioned that he would be vacating (with a man) to
Connecticut for a leisurely weekend while I had the apartment. The most stressful bit of the instructions he gave before
leaving was the lock and key situation, which was very hard
to master. You had to do it a specific way or you'd get locked
out. And given that he'd be in Connecticut, he couldn't just
run right over and save my ass. But still, it was a doorknob
keyhole. And I had the key. How hard could it really be?

In hindsight, I should have practiced while the owner
was still there, but instead I waited until he'd already been
gone for over an hour before I left the apartment. And even
though I had the keys in hand, I didn't remember how to
do the thing that would keep me from getting locked out.
So I got locked out. And how had this *happened*? Moments
before I'd been chilling on the sofa with my feet up eating a
cupcake. How could I get back to *that*? How could I do this
over and end up not locked out?

Calling the owner felt too humiliating, but I don't know what I was waiting for. He was only getting further and further away from the city. And I had no other option. There's no sugar-coating how upset he was to learn he'd have to get off his Connecticut-bound train, board one in the opposite direction, save my ass, and then start the journey to Connecticut all over again. Or how upset he *still* was when he arrived and exasperatingly re-showed me how to trick the knob into working properly. In my defense, it really shouldn't have been so hard. But in his defense, I was a stupid girl from suburbia ruining his weekend getaway.

For my next trip I ventured over to the Upper East Side and found the nicest place yet, a high-ceilinged studio a few blocks from Bloomingdale's. I loved the apartment so much that I stayed there three different times, texting the owner directly when I was planning a trip. The owner, a single woman in her fifties, was loud and a bit boisterous, but very kind, always leaving flowers or a note to welcome me when I stayed. She even called to let me know I'd left a necklace behind and then mailed it back to me.

I was never sure where she went when her apartment was rented, just as I was never sure what she kept in the closet that remained locked while she was away. I do know her top dresser drawer contained a book about sex and her medicine cabinet was so unorganized that I wasn't sure if what I took when I had a headache was ibuprofen or not. One night a cockroach skittered across the floor, a bit disturbing in such an upscale apartment, and all night I wondered if there were more hiding beneath boxes or couches. I also wondered if she knew there were cockroaches.

See, these are the things you wonder about people whose lives you become privy to. Even if only for a matter of days, you are standing in for someone else. You are you, but as them. And you suddenly know so much about the way a complete stranger lives his or her life. So then, can you really consider them strangers?

Once I moved to Manhattan, my new model New Yorkers became my landlord and her husband, who lived across the hall from me in a studio apartment the same size as mine. They were oddballs, to be sure. Hippie types. I loved this about them, and the free spirited way they lived their simple lives. Sometimes they'd come home from an event a bit drunk, stumbling through the halls, helping each other up the stairs, laughing, and she took such good care of my cat when I was away that I sometimes worried I'd return to find my cat now living across the hall and unwilling to come back home.

They owned their apartment as well as mine and sometimes chose to keep the extra apartment empty. And I liked picturing my apartment that way, as an art studio where my landlord could paint and house her museum pieces. Where she could look out onto the courtyard, drink a bottle of wine with her husband, and then stumble across the hall late at night, returning to the tiny sanctuary of space that was their own.

GOING

BEING GIVEN THE GO~AHEAD TO WORK MY
current job remotely, the next most pressing matter on my
Moving to New York Checklist was finding a place to live.
Trust me, this was just as daunting to me as the New York
City job market, perhaps even more so.

Because I'd heard many things about housing in
Manhattan. Not only that it was ridiculously expensive,
but also that it was ridiculously hard to find. Not that there
weren't good options, but that these options were few and far
between, requiring a sometimes lengthy and always intense
search to find those diamonds among the realty rough. And
not actually living in New York put me at a definite disadvan-
tage, in that when apartments became available, they were
usually snatched up right away. And being in Cleveland

meant I couldn't just cab it over to check the place out, put down a deposit, and sign the contract.

I decided the only way I was going to find a decent place without actually being there was to hire a real estate broker. You hear about brokers a lot when you talk apartments in New York City. It's a great way to go if you want to significantly up your chances of finding a nice place. But it comes at a cost. Most brokers charge 15 to 20 percent of an entire year's rent for their services. Meaning if the dream apartment your broker finds will cost you $2,500 a month, then in addition to handing $7,500 over to your new landlord for the security deposit and first and last month's rent, you'll also be cutting a check for up to $6,000 to your broker, just for finding you the place.

Trust me. I badly wanted to save that broker money. But I didn't see how else I was going to find an apartment, especially from a distance. So I got a recommendation of a popular broker and booked a weekend trip the month before I was set to move. I told the broker the kinds of properties I was interested in seeing while I was in town, and although it meant I'd be paying him handsomely, I spent my nights dreaming about my future apartment in the city. I couldn't wait to walk through each option my broker was lining up for me, to look out the windows, stand in the sunlight, listen to the traffic at the nearest intersection and see if I could picture myself taking up residence in any of those exact spots.

I met my broker on a Saturday morning at a Starbucks off of Columbus and 81st Street. As he opened his laptop and began to walk me through various tricks and tips of New York real estate, it became evident that while I'd been incredibly clear in my correspondence with him, he'd somehow missed the memo about me actually wanting to *see properties* while in town.

I mean, what the hell else was I doing here?

This was, in fact, my *only* opportunity to see properties, and while I was pleasant in my dismissal of his gross error, inside I was fuming. More than that, I was freaking out. Here I was, in town to house hunt, and I didn't have a single appointment.

My broker made some calls and was able to arrange a last-minute viewing for me of an apartment in Kip's Valley, around 23rd Street. I was already in a bad mood, but the street didn't inspire much confidence. It struck me as mean, dirty, and a little unsafe. Standing in the apartment looking out the window, I didn't like it. I didn't like how it made me feel. I couldn't picture myself living there. Plus, it was so damn small. A studio with only a few steps of living room, even fewer steps of kitchen, a small bathroom, and a closet. I tried to stay positive, reasoning that the place surely looked a thousand times better with furniture, and it was then that I remembered seeing something about a "furnished" option available on the listing as we were driving over. Meaning if I paid more in rent, they'd provide furniture.

"If I chose the furnished option, what would the apartment come with?" I asked the property manager who'd let us in.

"This," he answered, pointing to an old, dirty, love-seat-sized couch currently sitting against one wall.

Unappealing as this whole situation was, the thought occurred to me that maybe this was as good as it gets. Maybe this was New York City living. Maybe I could visit a hundred apartments and they'd all pretty much have these same components. Small. Ugly. Bad views of mean streets. I asked my broker for his opinion on whether this was a good option, and of course he said it was. A *great deal*. An *amazing location*. But his motives were surely insincere. He wanted my money. I didn't want to give it to him, especially after he'd royally botched my house-hunting trip. Mostly though, I just didn't see how I could live in a place that didn't inspire any kind of excitement or wistful imaginings when I thought of my future in it.

So I passed. I said goodbye to my worthless broker and took the subway back to the apartment I was renting for the weekend. It's an apartment I'd rented before. Near Lexington and 62nd Street, it was on the Upper East Side, and I loved the location. I loved its proximity to the sparkling lights cascading down the sides of Bloomingdales. And I loved the apartment itself. Still a studio, this one was open, light, and had high ceilings. It had a cheery feel, not to mention a more modern and upkept one. In short, this was exactly the kind of apartment I was hoping to find.

Left to my own apartment-finding devices, I turned to Craigslist. In my defense, I'd used Craigslist when I moved to Cleveland after graduate school, and the house I'd found was as darling as it was perfect. Almost seven years later, I was still in that same house. Honestly, I was sad to now be leaving it, even for New York.

Hoping Craigslist had one more miracle property with my name on it, I opened a new search. Since I planned to sell my furniture and move very minimally, I was ideally looking for a place that was furnished—with more than a dirty loveseat. Also one that allowed a cat, had relatively flexible lease terms, and, perhaps most importantly, was having an open house that very day so I could come look at it. With those filters set, I pushed the search button.

In a city of eight million people, only one apartment matched my search.

One.

I called and made an appointment and then began walking uptown.

Much like my weekend rental, the one apartment that turned up on my search was also on the Upper East Side, only much farther east. Almost as far east as you can get without falling into the actual East River. Between 1st and York Avenues, as soon as I turned onto 78th Street I could feel my hopes rising, despite my best efforts to keep them grounded based on the apartment I'd seen earlier in the day. But this was a different part of town. This was a *totally* different part of town. And things here were quieter. And much prettier. A tree-lined street. Lovely brick buildings. And when from the other side of the street I saw a darling bright red door, I remember thinking to myself, "*If this apartment is in that building, then I want it.*"

The apartment was indeed in the red-doored building.

I went through the red door and up the two flights of stairs to apartment 3C. I stepped inside and knew immediately that it was perfect.

It was just as small as the apartment I'd seen earlier, maybe even a little smaller. At 350 square feet, it was basically just a single rectangular room. A bathroom immediately on the right when you first walked in, a closet on the left, a small kitchenette on the right after passing the bathroom (a hotel-sized mini fridge, a sink, and the smallest oven you've ever seen), a living area in the center that held a TV on top of a dresser across from an oversized loveseat-style chair for one, a double bed against the back wall, and a small desk set up in front of the window, at the foot of the bed.

This may sound sparsely furnished, but remember, we're only talking about 350 square feet. Smaller than most people's living room. So that's actually quite a bit of furniture (a bed!) for a living room. Needless to say, it was cozy. But it was also charming. And I'm not just saying that. The lamp set up on the desk, the reindeer wood carving above the hearth, the retro bedspread. Even the mismatched set of kitchen utensils hanging on the wall struck me as charming. The mismatched sets of *everything* (sheets, towels, dishes) that had been collected and carefully preserved over the years by a very attentive landlord.

The landlord, a tall, slender woman in her fifties with a very artsy vibe, asked me a few questions and took notes as I looked out the window and peeked inside of closets, and it was hard to tell whether the things I was saying were helping or hurting me. No, I didn't currently live in New York. Yes, I was single. No, I didn't smoke. Yes, I had a cat. I left the apartment unsure of my chances but positive that I wanted it. Not only because I literally had no other options, but also because it was so perfect. And I'd known it immediately. It had the unmistakable feel of a writer's apartment.*

I had grand intentions of playing hard to get if the

---

*I learned later that the tenant who was moving out was indeed a writer, and she'd just landed her first book deal.

landlord offered me the apartment. "I'll sleep on it," or something like that, but instead I responded right away and told her that I'd take it. The landlord and her husband met me at a restaurant across from my rented apartment on 62nd Street the next morning and I signed the contract. As I handed over a check for the first month's rent, a whopping $2350, a part of me did wonder if the whole thing was a scam. I mean, those things happened right? Clueless girls who came to the city and didn't know any better?

But I trusted the landlord and her husband implicitly, and not just because they had a cat named after a Counting Crows song who they couldn't wait to introduce to my own cat. (An intra-building feline romance!) No, it was more than the cat. I trusted these people because they'd lived in their apartment, the one just across the hall from mine, for 30 years, the bulk of their lives. Shared, accumulated, grown over three decades as a couple in the same 350-square-foot space. It simply didn't seem possible, which is why I liked them. I liked them for proving wrong the insistence of every suburbia couple I'd ever known that more is better; that more is, in fact, essential to one's very existence as a person.

And so I didn't worry about the fate of my check or my personal information as I left it in their hands that morning over an outdoor table and empty coffee cups and flew back to Cleveland. All I felt was an overwhelming sense of relief that I'd accomplished what I'd set out to. I'd found an apartment in Manhattan. A darling, charming one owned by cat-loving artsy minimalist hippies. And I'd found it all by myself.

COMING

I SPENT MY LAST NEW YORK CITY SUNSET AT the top of Rockefeller Center watching the contrast deepen between the night and the lighted little squares of the Empire State Building's windows. It was dazzling, every time I saw it. Especially tonight, when the question of when I would see it again was not one I could answer.

It had been a day of favorite things. Bread and cheese from Greenwich Village eaten on a bench at Washington Square Park. My favorite Harlem pizzeria. One final oatmeal raisin cookie from Levain. The garden at St. Luke's church, a favorite hideaway of mine. I loved watching people among the benches and flowers, imagining what had brought each person to that same garden.

If anyone had glanced over at my mother that day, lying

233

across one of the shady benches and solidly asleep, they'd have seen a woman who'd flown in to help move her daughter across the country. We were California bound in the morning, heading toward my new job and my new house. One that had a bedroom. And a washer and dryer I wouldn't have to schlep all my underwear down the street in order to use.

Mom had been blessed with the gift of being able to nap on command, a trait I had not inherited, and as she slept amidst the trees and flower bushes, I thought she looked quite angelic. My angel mother, truly, and my gratitude for her help over those next several days stirred a swelling of daughterly love. If anyone glanced over at my mother that day, I hope that's what they saw.

As for what people may have thought to look over at *me* that day, I couldn't have said. What even would *I* have said, knowing the truth? What exactly was it that had brought me here? What series of decisions had led me to discover this garden the previous year? And what seed within me had felt I'd needed to settle in this city in the first place? Perhaps most importantly to me, how much of my life had I spent nurturing this seed—a seed of hope and possibility, of dreams and potential—and had I stayed long enough for any of this to have come to fruition?

I loved New York, certainly, but I suspected anyone playing the game I was playing would have deduced from one look that I was aching to leave. They would have seen that on my way to the garden that very day, I'd felt hot and embarrassed over a man's asking, "Who let all the lesbians out?" when he saw me and my pixie cut approaching from the other direction. Embarrassed to have been incorrectly labeled, and even more so that the mislabeling had bothered me so much. Or at all. And they also would have seen, in trance-like, flash-forward style, the moment later that night at the top of 30 Rock when the tourist who refused to move from his perch in front of the coveted gap between the thick reflective slabs of plastic railing turned to pick a fight, me once again getting hot with bother and annoyance.

"You're hogging the crack! Others are waiting!" I cried out, rather desperately. This was, after all, my last night in New York.

"Yeah, well I've waited too. I've waited all day. And I can stay here as long as I want," he replied.

And how odd, to know with certainly that what you need most in the world is a little more space—or at least a little more space between you and the idiot next to you—even as you're taking in the best view of your favorite building in the world. I mean, how do you turn away from that?

I did, eventually, and my final subway ride was to the car rental place the following morning, which saw me laughably driving my rented minivan back uptown. I'd never been behind the wheel while living in Manhattan, and I'd literally prayed for there to be an open place to park along the street once I returned. There was, and I slid in, loaded up, and drove away within the hour, my cat hiding between boxes, my mom wielding navigation from the passenger seat.

My friend Molly was there to help, and she filmed the exodus, my minivan pulling away from the sidewalk and ultimately disappearing around the corner. I watched the video over and over again, the street where I lived shady from trees, focused on the now-empty parking spot.

To me it was proof that I had been there.

Going

I'D SAY I MOVED TO NEW YORK CITY BECAUSE OF a boy, but that's not really how it happened. That isn't the whole story, anyway. Not to mention it belittles my actual motivation for moving there, which was that I really wanted to. I always had. I was one of those wide-eyed silly girls who always thought of Manhattan in a sort of wistful, romantic way, as if it were the kind of place where dreams couldn't help but come true.

I'd vacationed there a lot over the years, usually to attend a class required for my gemology diploma, and I'd always tack a few days onto one end of the trip so I could have fun and explore the city. And thus the mammoth NYC Pull began to burrow its way into my heart, causing me to tilt my head slightly when contemplating its boroughs. I may have even begun permanently leaning to one side, or at least I was left with the sensation I was leaning, so great was the NYC Pull's cumulative effect. If I saw a show I liked, tasted goods at a delicious bakery, stayed out until 3:00 in the morning and then exited the 23rd Street subway station to find the Empire State Building's gloriously lighted halo staring me in the face, joined the throngs of subway commuters purposefully sipping coffee while reading the paper and doing it all while balancing on precariously high heels, I would feel almost bowled over by the need to be a part of it all. I mean, who wouldn't *love* this?

But wistful as I may have been, I was also rational. I figured New York City had its fair share of downsides, too. Though I hadn't felt even the slightest bit tired of it during any of my visits, I reasoned that the constant presence of other people—the dense, suffocating *masses* of people—would at some point grow tiring. The filth, the lack of open spaces, the stench of summertime, the heaps of trash. The unfortunate and downtrodden asking for money on every corner, the void of peace and quiet, the exorbitant cost of living. Wouldn't *all* of that grow tiring? I mean, these are not little things.

So I went to the source.

By source I mean the only people I really knew who were full-on Manhattanites. A former business school classmate of mine, we hadn't exactly been chummy, but I asked him and his wife if they wanted to meet for dinner during one of my trips. I tried to explain my crush on Manhattan lightly, so as not to sound like the stalker that I surely was, and as I voiced my hesitant but hopeful admission that my future career ambition (gemology) might soon have me relocating to New York, I confessed that I did wonder how living in the city would compare with simply vacationing there. And so I asked them, sure to prime them by bringing up the trash and filth and noise in the verbiage of my questioning, I told them there simply *had* to be things they didn't like about living in New York City.

What happened next is a moment so moving that I hope both of them someday include it in their own memoirs. They turned their heads toward one another, a dreamy look passing between them, and then turned back to me.

"There's nothing we don't like about living here," my former classmate replied.

"We don't ever want to leave," his wife said immediately, even as she clutched her nine-months-pregnant belly, about to drive home on the back of the motorized scooter that was their sole source of transportation.

And these lines stuck with me. I couldn't shake them, but who *could*? Such bold declarations. Such unadulterated devotion. And from a couple both far from their western families, each admitting that despite the distance between them and their loved ones, they hoped nothing would ever part them from the city.

So I wasn't imagining it then, this hold that New York can have over people, and clearly did.

But life is funny. Funny meaning it usually gets kind of mixed up. Things happening in the wrong order, things coming from left field, things both sucking harder and burning brighter than you ever would have imagined in the uneducated, naïve versions of life you spend your childhood — and most of your twenties, too — planning.

I mentioned there was a boy, and there was one. Because instead of make a life for myself in the big city, I went and fell in love with a boy from Ohio and was happily planning a future with him in the Midwest. The possibility of New York couldn't hold a candle to the reality of how happy this Cleveland man made me, which is why when he showed up at my house one day to drop the "I don't think I can marry you" bomb, I wasn't thinking, "*Well, at least now I can move to New York.*" It was more like, "*There goes my life.*" But when I had recovered enough from the loss to contemplate my next move—literal as well as figurative—New York City beckoned. I took my broken heart and got out of Dodge.

So, yeah, you can say it's because of a boy if that's how you want to read it. And I wouldn't be ashamed if New York only happened for me because Plan A fell apart. After all, if you're going to have a Plan B, New York City is one hell of a backup.

About the Author

TALI NAY ALWAYS WANTED TO BE A FICTION writer and was thus surprised when "real life" is what came out when she actually sat down to write something substantial. Tali studied writing in college, and then—entirely by accident—found herself working in business. She went on to earn an MBA, although has since left Corporate America in order to pursue her dream of becoming a gemologist. After a stint in New York City earning her diploma at GIA, Tali now works in the gemology industry and lives in San Diego, California. You can follow her at talinaybooks.com.

Made in the USA
Coppell, TX
04 January 2020

14101317R00146